D. P. LEINSTER-MACKAY

The Educational World of Daniel Defoe

EℓS

English Literary Studies

University of Victoria

1981

ENGLISH LITERARY STUDIES
Published at the University of Victoria

GENERAL EDITOR
Samuel L. Macey

ISBN 0-920604-44-7

The ELS Monograph Series is published in consultation with members of the Department by ENGLISH LITERARY STUDIES, Department of English, University of Victoria, B.C., Canada.

ELS Monograph Series No. 23
© 1981 by D. P. Leinster-Mackay

To my Mother and Father

CONTENTS

ACKNOWLEDGEMENTS

I wish to acknowledge the signal encouragement and generous research funding by the Education Department of the University of Western Australia in my research for this monograph.

Mrs. Elizabeth Sarfaty was my assiduous research assistant; Miss Marie Charles and Miss Ebe Dolzadelli my indefatigable typists; and Dr. John Hay, Dr. Laadan Fletcher, Dr. Michael Herriman and my wife Mrs. Jewel Leinster-Mackay, my helpful readers and critics. I am very grateful to all of them for their help but I claim responsibility for any imperfections — hopefully few — remaining in the text.

CHAPTER 1

The Extent of Defoe's Educational Writings

In November 1893, a committee of teachers presented to the School Board of Würzburg a curriculum and time-table for adoption by the elementary schools under its aegis. This curriculum and time-table was based on Herbart-Ziller principles involving the 'Dual theory of the Historical Culture epochs and Concentration centres'.[1] In accordance with the rigid dictates of this nineteenth-century school curriculum the children in the municipal elementary schools of Würzburg were to have studied *Robinson Crusoe* extensively in their second year had the plan been adopted. Crusoe was to have been introduced, in project-like fashion, into their natural history, geography, reading, writing and composition, in their singing and even into their arithmetic. In the event the proposals were not implemented.

The proposed intensity of this study of *Robinson Crusoe* arose from a misguided adherence to partly misunderstood principles established by J. F. Herbart in his educational writings; but its very presence in the proposed curriculum in the first place could possibly be attributed to Rousseau. Was it not Rousseau after all who had pronounced on it so forthrightly in his *Emile*? Rousseau wrote:

> Since we must have books, there is one book which ... supplies the best treatise on an education according to nature. This is the first book Émile will read; for a long time it will form his whole library, and it will always retain an honoured place. ... What is this wonderful book? Is it Aristotle? Pliny? Buffon? No; it is Robinson Crusoe.[2]

No doubt Rousseau's acclaim helped to give to *Robinson Crusoe* a greater international dimension to what was already a popular book in England and France, Germany and Sweden. As the Rev. Mark Noble, an Anglican clergyman, affirmed in 1806, "I have never known but one person of sense who disliked it. Rousseau, and after him all France, applauded it."[3] The popularity of Crusoe in England is evidenced by its reaching four editions between the 25th April and the 8th August 1719 and by Defoe's production of a further volume, *The Farther Adventures of Robinson Crusoe*, on 20th August 1719, which in turn was followed by his *Serious Reflections during the Life and Surprizing Adventures of Robinson Crusoe* on the 6th August 1720. Defoe, ever an opportunist with an eye to a quick profit, cashed in on this popularity. Internationally, the ripples from Rousseau's comments may have contributed to the popularity of *Robinson Crusoe* and its translation into many languages including, according to John Robert Moore, an Eskimo translation published in a newspaper in Greenland more than a century ago.[4]

James Beattie (1735-1803), Professor of Moral Philosophy at Marischal College, was in agreement with Rousseau when he wrote in his *Dissertations Moral and Critical* that "this is one of the best books that can be put into the hands of children."[5] Similarly, Hugh Blair (1718-1800)—the Scottish divine and critic, Regius Professor of Rhetoric and Belles Lettres at Edinburgh from 1762—regarded *Robinson Crusoe* as "very useful instruction."[6] Showing acute Rousseauvian perception, Walter Wilson (1781-1847), the nineteenth-century historian of the dissenting churches, averred in his *Memoirs of the Life and Times of Daniel Defoe* (1830):

> As a work of amusement, it is one of the first books put into the hands of youth; and there can be none more proper to insinuate instruction, whilst it administers delight.[7]

Sir Leslie Stephen (1832-1904), the celebrated editor of the *Dictionary of National Biography*, increased the number of these generous encomia when he wrote about *Robinson Crusoe* that "to have pleased all the boys in England for near a hundred and fifty years is, after all, a remarkable feat."[8] Acknowledgements of the value of *Robinson Crusoe* are legion, and it is not surprising, therefore, that it was given as earliest reading to boys like George Borrow, the later Scottish Victorian novelist[9] and [Sir] Walter Besant,[10] later fellow novelist and writer on the eighteenth century. *Robinson Crusoe* found a special place even in the otherwise academic and formal education of John Stuart Mill. He wrote in his *Autobiography*:

> Of children's books . . . I had scarcely any, except an occasional gift from a relation or acquaintance: among those I had, Robinson Crusoe was preeminent, and continued to delight me through all my boyhood.[11]

Rousseau, in his *Emile*, had recognized the value of *Robinson Crusoe* on the criterion of utility. It was a book which upheld true value, according to Rousseau, since it emphasized the need for the 'practical' as opposed to the 'decorative.' Society had inverted its values and Crusoe provided a homeostatic device to correct this persistent error, in the impressionable young. Certainly an examination of *Robinson Crusoe* in the twentieth century shows it not only to have a differing *Weltanschauung* or world-view with its religious and devout underpinning but also to be strongly oriented towards praise for the practical. What is the use of Greek and Latin compared with carpentry and pottery on a desert island? The satisfaction which Defoe evinced with the practical is evident in *Robinson Crusoe* when he wrote:

> I had never handled a tool in my life; and yet in time, by labour, application, and contrivance, I found at last that I wanted nothing but I could have made it especially if I had the tools.[12]

In his expression of such sentiment, Defoe was contributing to the evolving educational debate, which goes back to Aristotle, concerning the relative merits of a liberal and vocational education. He seems to be more pedagogically conscious, however, when he writes later about Crusoe's instruction of Man Friday:

> I was greatly delighted with him, and made it my business to teach him everything that was proper to make him useful, handy, and helpful.[13]

Those who turn to *Robinson Crusoe*, however, in the wake of Rousseau's recommendation are likely to be disappointed if they hope to discern in it an educational treatise of any import. Apart from the basic principle of a 'natural' education, which in any case is stated *en passant* rather than argued cogently, and two or three examples of didacticism, there is little to cause the student of educational thought to agree roundly with Rousseau, despite Crusoe's statement that,

> I was yet but a very sorry workman, though time and necessity made me a complete natural mechanic soon after, as I believe it would do anyone else.[14]

The asseveration of even the universal application of this educational principle does not necessarily make *Robinson Crusoe* educationally significant. Consequently doubt is left in the mind about the possible value of Daniel Defoe as an educational thinker and writer. It is the purpose of this book, therefore, to determine the nature and assess the value of Defoe's contribution to education. Such an undertaking can be very adequately justified by reference to the historiography of education where it is difficult to find even brief references to Defoe. No mention is made of him in W. Boyd and E. J. King, *The History of Western Education* (1972), or in Gerald Gutels, *A History of the Western Educational Experience* (1972), or in Robert Ulich, *History of Educational Thought* (1968), or in S. J. Curtis, *History of Education in Great Britain* (1967) or even in a work by Philip J. Greven, with the promising title *Child-rearing Concepts, 1628-1861—Historical Sources* (1973). S. J. Curtis and M. E. A. Boultwood, in their *A Short History of*

Educational Ideas (1966), examine simplistically the ideas of John Locke in Chapter X and those of Rousseau in Chapter XI, but find no room for a mention of Defoe or any of his contemporaries who had valuable insights to offer on education. Adolphe Meyer, in *An Educational History of the Western World* (1972) refers once to Defoe but only in the context of the commercial revolution in the eighteenth century in which Defoe played a part. T. L. Jarman, in *Landmarks in the History of Education* (1963), makes only one reference, viz., to Defoe's attendance at Newington Green Academy. Similarly J. W. Adamson in *A Short History of Education* (1922) alludes once only to Defoe giving no clue, for example, as to the value of Defoe's contemporary observation on both the dissenting academies and charity schools. Such an oversight is evident also in E. P. Cubberley *The History of Education* where reference is made to *Robinson Crusoe* but only to its being England's first novel. W. H. G. Armytage in *Four Hundred Years of English Education* (1964) is more generous in his comment, but even Armytage, customarily esoteric in his educational allusions, refers to Defoe only three times. Admittedly one of these references is to Defoe's *Giving Alms no Charity* (1704), a work which concerned itself partly with workhouse children and partly with attacking Sir Humphrey Mackworth, Member of Parliament and co-founder of the Society for Promoting Christian Knowledge (S.P.-C.K.). Nevertheless, Armytage could be included in a general comment that Defoe has been neglected by writers of general histories of education.

Historians of education who have written specifically about eighteenth-century education have, on the other hand, recognized the value of Defoe as a source of contemporary comment. M. G. Jones, in *The Charity School Movement in the Eighteenth Century* (1938), alluded to Defoe and his great law of subordination as well as referring to him several times in connection with education in the course of her definitive work on the Charity Schools. Likewise H. Maclachlan,[15] Irene Parker[16] and J. W. Ashley Smith[17] all recognize in Defoe a potential contemporary witness to the Dissenting Academies and in particular to the academy at Newington Green, run by Dr. Charles Morton.

If we recognize then, that in the past Defoe has been minimally used by specialists writing on education in the eighteenth century but otherwise overlooked almost completely by the majority of historians of education, it becomes a matter of importance if in fact Defoe had something worthwhile to say on education. The researcher into Defoe and education is faced with a monumental task since Defoe was one of the most prolific writers in English literature, putting his hand to poetry, history, biography, political polemics and pamphleteering, novels, religious tracts and, over a long period of time, journalism. During his life, Defoe wrote more than five hundred separate works ranging from slender pamphlets to weighty volumes. Of these, some forty works concern themselves with education in some degree, written over a period of more than thirty years from 1697 to his death in 1731. (A list of these, with full titles, is given in the Appendix.) In this respect Defoe differs from others like Quintilian, Montaigne, Locke and Kant who have written about education but whose educational ideas can be gauged by reference to only a few works. Because of his essays and educational comment spread over so many years, there could be difficulties involved in consistency, in collation and in analysis. Surprisingly, and unlike in Rousseau himself, there are few, if any, inconsistencies in Defoe's thinking. Throughout his writing he displays a sound appreciation of the value of education itself and of the importance of moral training in the early years. As is seen in *Defoe on Education*,[18] inconsistency of thinking is not so much a weakness of Defoe's writing as is the repetitious overstatement of a position: such weaknesses are almost mutually exclusive. Problems of collation and analysis arise from the heterogeneous collection of works which make up this educational 'credo' to be found scattered through his writings. These range from poetry to didactic and moralistic works and from fictional novels to socio-political tracts examining very real situations. Defoe has been described by more than one critic[19] as a 'polygrapher' which is a useful term to cover the various literary forms in which Defoe engaged. Such a recognition of these various literary forms could lead to categorizing Defoe by way of differing roles. His works could be examined under such headings as the *relator* (his novels), the *recorder* (histories and biography), the *projector* (his education schemes contained in both books and pamphlets), the *instructor* (his didactic works) and the *educator* (where his main task appears to be laying down educational principles). Such a mode of categorization, however, would lead to a very great imbalance amongst the several parts. It becomes necessary, therefore, to adopt another paradigm of analysis. One that lends itself to a gradual and methodical exegesis of Defoe's 'educational' works is that of considering first those where Defoe is concerned with criticizing existing practice; secondly, those where Defoe is seen to be defending an institution, giving advice or evincing an intelligent interest in any aspect of education; and thirdly, those where he is expressing educational tenets or stating an educational position. The three categories might respectively be termed 'criticism,' 'advocacy' and 'tenets' or 'beliefs.' It is readily recognized that such a paradigm leads to problems in so far as, in the first place, parts of certain works could be subsumed under one or more categories, and in the second place, it is possible to regard 'criticism' of existing practice as the obverse of an educational 'tenet.' Nevertheless, despite these possible difficulties it is intended to adopt this paradigm for analysing Defoe's writings, but first it will be necessary to place these writings in their historical context of late Stuart and early Hanoverian England, including the educational context of early popular education and the challenge of the dissenting academies to the universities and endowed grammar schools. It will be necessary, moreover, to examine Defoe's life, however sketchily, in order to give contextual meaning to the writings themselves. Chapter 2 is devoted to these tasks.

CHAPTER 2

Defoe and His England

There are intrinsic difficulties in adapting G. M. Trevelyan's periodic concept of 'Defoe's England'[1] to describe the expanded period from the date of Defoe's birth, probably in 1660, to Defoe's death in 1731. First, such a period spans over seventy years which, from the Restoration (1660) to the Treaty of Vienna (1731), saw enormous changes which are difficult to encompass within the confines of a single epithet. Secondly, Defoe was really only an active participant in that England from about 1685 onwards when, as a young and newly married man, he rode out to help the Duke of Monmouth in his ill-fated rebellion. On the other hand, it could be argued that an understanding of England in the late 1660's and 1670's is necessary if Defoe's dissenting background and education are to be considered in their full context. Despite these difficulties it is proposed to examine England of the late Stuart and early Hanoverian period as an integrated whole. It is readily recognized nevertheless, that such an intention does entail the juxtaposing of a seventeenth-century - eighteenth-century context which in part at least seems static, and not moving on a time-continuum, with an exegesis of Defoe's life which by comparison is dynamic, moving indirectly but inexorably from Cripplegate, where he was born, to Bunhill Fields nearby where he was buried. This chapter will, therefore, attempt two tasks, viz., (1) a social, political, religious and educational analysis of late Stuart and early Hanoverian England with reference to Defoe being made, where appropriate; and (2) a brief complementary exegesis of Defoe's life.

The Monarchy

Perhaps the most important single factor in any consideration of England after 1660, was the continuation of the institution of the monarchy after the interregnum years of the Commonwealth. During the late Stuart and early Hanoverian period, the monarchy experienced moments of crisis and periods of stability. Charles II was, no doubt, determined not to 'go on his travels again' and with a combination of cunning toleration, moderation and intrigue he skilfully steered the newly re-furbished English monarchy through choppy waters. With the aid of the wise counsel of Edward Hyde, Earl of

Clarendon, and later the secret French funding, Charles II was able to give the institution of the monarchy twenty-five years of renewed existence before it was openly challenged on his death when his Roman Catholic brother James, Duke of York, became King James II.

The death of Charles, filial ambition and the well-known religious predilections of James II precipitated the rebellion in 1685 of the Duke of Monmouth, Charles II's natural son, whose venture ended in disaster at Sedgemoor in Somerset. Daniel Foe (as he was generally known till about 1703 and even sometimes afterwards) took part in this rebellion but after the defeat of the rebel army, Defoe managed to escape capture, and a likely death.

The Catholic policies of James II were not altogether antagonizing. In order to free Catholics from the restrictions of the penal code James attempted to extend the principle of toleration to Dissenter and Catholic alike. Such a pre-meditated action was the occasion for Defoe's first essay at political pamphleteering when, in 1687, refusing to be hoodwinked he opposed James II's policy of religious indemnity.

It was not surprising, therefore, to find Defoe in the van of support for William of Orange when the latter made a bid for the English throne in the Bloodless Revolution in 1688. This political revolution, which established the reign of William III and Mary, was in reality a social revolution that confirmed a new social order, with the English nobility and gentry consolidating their position on the losses sustained by the monarchy. With the constitutional nature of the new monarchy assured, the aristocracy and gentry increased their wealth and power, the rationale for which constitution was to be found in John Locke's *Treatise on Civil Government*. For Defoe, the reign of William gave happy days and marked the beginning of his life-long association with successive monarchs and governments. As a fervent supporter of William III, Defoe had occasion to defend him against criticism, which he did successfully with his satirical poem in rhyming couplets, *The True-Born Englishman* (1701). That poem, which deeply ingratiated Defoe with William, left his fortunes high and the door open to the counsels of the King. At this triumphal point in Defoe's career, the accidental death of William III and the accession of Queen Anne led to a drastic change of fortune and a more precarious existence.

The accession of Anne did not augur well for Defoe. She was an Anglican supporter, indeed she was the only fervently Anglican monarch for over a century (as Donald Greene has pointed out). But before her reign the Hanoverian succession had been determined by the Act of Settlement of 1701. If the purpose of this Act had been to discourage Jacobite ambitions, it had the

16

very opposite effect on James, the Old Pretender, and son of the exiled James II who had died in that year. Anne's reign was characterized by continental war and domestic fears of Jacobite risings. These fears and the oscillating fortunes of Whigs and Tories during the Queen's reign were the determining factors in Defoe's employment by successive governments, despite his own dissenting and therefore *outré* background. Such was Harley's policy to make use of the fertile brains of publicists or writers that at one stage both Swift and Defoe were engaged by him in the service of the Queen. The Hanoverian succession, though enacted by a Tory administration, found Defoe serving the Tory Earl of Oxford, Robert Harley, when Anne died. Therefore Defoe was backing the wrong horse in view of the Tories' later associations with the Jacobite cause. This situation was a setback to Defoe's career.[2]

The ensuing period from 1714 to 1760 has been styled the 'Whig Supremacy'[3] during which period Tory politicians like Oxford and Bolingbroke[4] were eclipsed, being either exiled or imprisoned. Defoe experienced a similar eclipse but when finally released from prison he served as a double agent for his new Whig masters. Defoe showed thereby the capacity for survival for which he has been called a time-server. Certainly there are startling similarities between Defoe and the Vicar of Bray.[5] Although Defoe could boast of having in his possession the handwriting of four English monarchs,[6] he would seem to have had little contact with the German-speaking Hanoverians, George I and George II. Nevertheless, he remained in the service of the Whigs, and therefore the Hanoverian monarchy, till shortly before his death. The tenuous nature of the English constitution had given Defoe during his life-time much opportunity to take part in public affairs and much scope for his busy pen.

The Aristocracy and Gentry

In the pyramidical society of the late seventeenth and early eighteenth centuries, the aristocracy and gentry occupied a powerful position beneath the monarchy. Only a minority of nobles could trace their nobility back further than the Reformation, i.e., the Henrician sixteenth-century social revolution. There was a tendency for many individuals, through a process of upward social mobility, to be ennobled because of services rendered or wealth attained. Wealthy merchants, successful advocates and victorious generals and admirals tended, therefore, to join the spiritual peers to form the House of Lords. With an aristocracy that was open, largely determined by either wealth, or political and social achievement rather than by heredity, Defoe might have gained entry to the English aristocracy but for the premature death of William III. As it happened, Defoe was acquainted with some of the peerage, viz., the Earl of Oxford and Earl Godolphin, but only in the capacity of hireling: he shared their counsels but not their quality of esteem. Throughout much of his life, probably, Defoe entertained thoughts of being an English gentleman. Evidence for this is to be seen in his tendency to dress like a dandy, as for example in the portrait which forms the frontispiece of his poem *Jure Divino* (1706) and in the coat-of-arms he displayed on his personal coach in his more prosperous days. His preoccupation with the education of the gentry will be discussed in the next chapter. Meanwhile it is sufficient to note that through his family and scholastic background, Defoe had much leeway to make up before achieving the status of 'gentleman.' This deficiency may account for his extreme criticism of the education of the English gentleman. On the other hand, however, the country gentry were generally ignorant as well as boorish, as epitomized by Fielding's Squire Western or Goldsmith's Tony Lumpkin, so that Defoe was not alone in his critical view of the country-gentry's lack of education.

The Middling Ranks of Society

Below the aristocracy and gentry in the social pyramid were the middling ranks or orders of society who were, through trade, commerce and industry, to transform England into an industrial nation over the next one hundred and fifty years. In the process they were to raise their sights socially, seeking to set up their own family escutcheons based on their accumulated wealth. Defoe was a member of this middle stratum of society, being the son of a successful tallow-chandler and butcher. It was through his father's connections that he became a liveryman of the City of London. Although he was pejoratively called a 'hosier' by some of his critics[7] Defoe was in fact a hose-factor, i.e., a wholesaler rather than a retailer and as such had his fingers in this and several other trading and commercial pies. He had turned his back on a career in the Dissenting Minstry in order to enter trade and during his lifetime the author of *The Compleat English Tradesman* engaged in many commercial enterprises, some of which brought great profit and others, crippling debts. Defoe does represent, at the end of the seventeenth century, a new breed of men who in a rapidly expanding commercial world of foreign trade, invention and the Protestant ethic were to lay the foundations of Britain's greatness in the eighteenth and nineteenth centuries. They were to lay the foundations, too, of their own families' greatness. As Defoe wrote in *The Complete English Tradesman*, Vol. 1,

18

Trade is so far *here* from being inconsistent with a Gentleman, that *in short* trade in *England*, makes Gentlemen, and has peopled this nation with Gentlemen; for after a generation or two the tradesmen's children, or at least their grand-children, come to be as good Gentlemen, Statesmen, Parliament-men, Privy-Counsellors, Judges, Bishops, and Noblemen, as those of the highest birth and the most antient families.[8]

Defoe's life can be seen to coincide with that watershed in English history which saw the later stages of an expanding world;[9] colonial wars that needed financing but which brought rich rewards; important changes in agriculture known, by historians, as 'the agrarian revolution'; and the beginnings of Britain's industrial revolution, the roots of which were set in the early eighteenth century. These military, agricultural and industrial developments required capital. It is not surprising, therefore, that in the last decade of the seventeenth century two national institutions, the National Debt (1693) and the Bank of England (1694) were created. It was the 'Projecting Age,' as Defoe described it in *An Essay upon Projects* (1697), when inventive minds, combined with capitalist entrepreneurial skill, produced schemes which increased individual and national wealth. In *An Essay upon Projects* Defoe expounded on, *inter alia*, a Commission of Inquiry into Bankrupt Estates; on the founding of Friendly Societies; on a pension-office for the relief of the poor; on new methods of raising taxes and on nationalizing, through a royal pay-roll, the merchant seamen of Britain. Both in *An Essay upon Projects* and in his later work *Augusta Triumphans* (1728), Defoe suggested educational projects which required funding but which in due course would be beneficial to the nation. These educational investments included the founding of academies for training military officers, for cultivating musicians and for educating women. Viewed in this light the Society for Promoting Christian Knowledge, too, becomes a project of the greatest educational significance.

Two areas of human endeavour in the late seventeenth and early eighteenth centuries warranted its being called a projecting age. These were firstly the voyages of exploration which opened up new trading empires and secondly the study of natural science, which offered ingenious solutions to some of Man's continuing problems. Both these areas were subsumed within a popular concept in the eighteenth and later nineteenth centuries, "Man's Progress." Science and exploration were contributory factors leading to man's further progress. Such were the horizons and expectations of the middle ranks of the late Stuart and early Hanoverian society of which Defoe was an exemplar.

At the base of the societal pyramid were 'the lower orders' who formed the major groupings in society. This term was used to cover a wide range in society from the respectable, skilled mechanic to the dross of society which haunted the dens of London's underworld. The criminal underworld apart, the more fortunate anticipated a degree of deference from those beneath them. In the country such deference was accorded to the squire and the parson, the twin pillars of the 'establishment' in rural England. In the towns, still relatively small except for London, deference was based on a recognition of a differential in material wealth which separated one part of the nation from another. Few questioned this situation. It was ordained, and this was on the authority of Christ himself, that there would always be the poor. It was the duty of the Christian, if poor, to recognize this and if rich, to give to the poor to alleviate their lot. In the words of the eighteenth century hymn:

> The rich man in his castle
> The poor man at his gate
> God made them high and lowly
> And ordered their estate.

Charity was, therefore, an important issue in Defoe's England and one which Defoe, on more than one occasion, expatiated on, knowing it would interest his readers.[10] Similarly, the eighteenth-century social critic, Bernard Mandeville, knew that he would scandalize some of his readers by his *Fable of the Bees* or *Private Vices, Publick Benefits*. The prevailing view on Charity was based on what Defoe described as the *Great Law of Subordination* in a three-hundred page book of that title. It was necessary declared Defoe, if Society were to continue to function, for individuals 'to know their place' or 'their station.' This, of course, was the main educational aim of charity schools, to be discussed later.[11] Defoe was concerned with this 'categorical imperative' as is evinced by *The Behaviour of Servants in England* (1724?); *Everybody's Business is Nobody's Business* (1725) and *Servitude* (1729) in which he offers advice to servants.

Life in Defoe's England, among the lower orders, could be very coarse (as indeed it was among many country gentry) but it was also particularly wretched and squalid among the very poor of London. The dank, narrow streets of parts of metropolitan London were sinks of iniquity where thieves and prostitutes lurked to prey, in their different ways, on more respectable citizens. This was the London of Hogarth: it was also the London of Defoe, where gin was a general curse. Defoe, in his later life, inveighed against this aspect of society as is seen in *Some Considerations upon Street Walkers* (1726); in *Augusta Triumphans* which set out (a) 'to save our youth from Destruction, by clearing the streets of impudent *Strumpets*, suppressing *Gaming Tables* and *Sunday Debauches*' and (b) 'To save our lower Class of People from utter Ruin, and render them useful, by preventing the immoderate use of Geneva.' In the same year, he issued a pamphlet entitled *Street Robberies Considered*. His last recorded publication was, moreover, concerned with this aspect of life, in which he proposed *An Effectual Scheme, for the immediate Preventing of Street Robberies* (1730).

The Literati *and Coffee House Society*

The late seventeenth and early eighteenth centuries were a period of great contrasts. If ignorance and coarseness were marks of this exuberant age, classical scholarship and *finesse* were others. Such characteristics were to be found among the writers of the period, many of whom shared a common *Weltanschauung* based on a reverence for writings of Virgil, Cicero, Juvenal and Horace.[12] This world of polite learning was partly to be found in the coffee houses, or clubs (the English intellectual equivalent of the French salons), much frequented by *literati* like Steele and Addison, and of which there were about five hundred in Queen Anne's time. Coffee house or club society was where politicians and *literati*, among others, mingled together in equal social concourse and where wit and erudition were given full rein by an admiring audience.

In much the same way as French *philosophes* and *literati* during the reign of Louis XV and the oppression of *l'Ancien Régime* discussed concepts like Reason and Nature, so among the English *literati* there was a concern for similar considerations, perhaps best epitomized in Pope's *Essay on Man*, and in particular in the often quoted first two lines of his second epistle:

> Know then thyself, presume not God to scan,
> The proper study of mankind is man.

But these citizens of the world of polite learning—like Pope, Swift and Addison—were concerned also with their literary forms and with the relative values of ancient and modern writers. This battle between the Ancients and Moderns had been imported from France where Fontenelle's *Pluralité des Mondes* had excited the interest of Sir William Temple who then championed the Ancients by his *Essay upon the Ancient and Modern Learning* (1690). This defence of ancient learning was answered by William Wootton's *Reflections upon Ancient and Modern Learning* (1694) which led to the involvement in 1697 of Richard Bentley in this rather sterile and convoluted controversy. Jonathan Swift, who had been employed by Sir William Temple, contributed significantly to the controversy by his powerful satire on pedantry, *The Battel of the Books*, published in 1704. Defoe, who was outside the circle of Augustan writers,[13] could not be said to have had a personal interest in the controversy, since his knowledge of the Classics was regarded by the Augustans as minimal. Swift's personal slight of Defoe when he referred to him as an 'illiterate scribbler' exemplifies this contempt for his learning obtained from a dissenting academy. It was perhaps Defoe's scant knowledge of Latin that caused him to advocate the use of the vernacular and to doubt the value of ancient learning. In his *The Compleat English Gentleman* he wrote:

> We find the Moderns begin to gain upon the Antients extremely, and some parts of knowledge shine brighter in English than ever they did in Latin. Our phylosophers have exploded the Antients in many things, such as the mocion of the heavenly bodyes, the use of the magnet and the improvements of the navigacion which are all modern.[14]

This attack on the Ancients by Defoe would be almost certain to have been ignored by Augustan writers. Defoe was reckoned to be little more than a hack writer living near the denizens of Grub Street[15] and one who was to be found in Pope's *Dunciad*: "Earless on high stood unabashed De Foe, And Tutchin flagrant from the scourge below."[16] As such he was beneath the view of the Augustan *literati*.

Religion and the Church

If Defoe's contribution to the battle between the Ancients and Moderns would have been largely ignored, his religious and denominational views were not only well known but were at the heart of contemporary religious controversy. He could not be ignored in this religious context. His peculiar contribution to contemporary religious controversy was governed to a very large extent by his being brought up as a Dissenter, having Dissenting parents and a Dissenter's education. The refusal of Dissenting clergy to acknowledge the national church by swearing an oath in accordance with the Act of Uniformity (1662) incurred the hostility of the conforming clergy and led to deep religious divisions which were only exacerbated by the imposition of the Clarendon Code (1662-1665). These retaliatory measures gave much hardship to the Dissenters, and at the same time caused the development of their academies which began to appear in remote districts after the Act of Uniformity. Although the Toleration Act of 1689 removed many of the religious disabilities of the Dissenters, they were regarded still as being beyond the pale since, although the Occasional Conformity and Schism Acts were repealed in 1719, the Test and Corporation Acts, which forbade non-conformists taking public office, were not repealed till 1828. It was the practice of fellow non-conformists to conform occasionally in order to obtain public office: this practice was criticized by Defoe as 'playing Bo-peep with the Almighty.' Defoe's interest in the affairs of his co-religionists, excluding his satire *The Shortest Way . . .*, is indicated by his twenty-four booklets and pamphlets on the Dissenters, and a 352-pages volume, *The Present State of the Parties in Great Britain* (1712). His pen was particularly active in defence of Dissenters' education at the time of the Schism Act (1714), when he wrote no less than five pamphlets, making clear the nature of the threat to the Dissenters' religion by the curtailment of their education.

The Anglican church itself was divided into several factions after the accession of William and Mary. These divisions arose partly from Parliament's requiring all officials of Church and State to take the oaths of allegiance and supremacy. Archbishop Sancroft, six bishops and about four-hundred clergymen refused to take the oaths and were consequently deprived of their livings. These non-jurors upheld the doctrine of the Divine Right of Kings and were therefore 'constitutional heretics.'

The constitutionally minded William III had to rely for clerical support upon Latitudinarian clergy led by John Tillotson, who became Archbishop of Canterbury, and Gilbert Burnet, Bishop of Salisbury. Several bishoprics were filled by Whig adherents during William's reign who tended to increase the divisions in the church since so many of the parish clergy had Tory sympathies. This lack of co-operation between a largely Whig episcopate and a Tory-dominated Convocation led to the suppression of the latter in 1717, when it opposed the doctrines of religious liberty advocated by Hoadly, the Whig Bishop of Bangor. It was not till the second half of the nineteenth century, in 1853, that Convocation met again.

During the reign of Queen Anne there developed a new group of High Church Anglicans known as 'High Flyers' who attacked Dissenters, Low Churchmen, Latitudinarians and Whigs alike. These 'High Flyers,' who in the eighteenth century foreshadowed in some ways the Tractarians of the nineteenth century, were vocal in their criticism. None more so than Dr. Henry Sacheverell, Fellow of Magdalen College, Oxford. In 1709 he preached, before the Lord Mayor of London in St. Paul's Cathedral, a sermon, entitled: 'The Perils of False Brethren both in Church and State.' Not content with this Sacheverell had some forty-thousand copies of this sermon printed. Sacheverell was impeached for his inflammatory sermon. This precipitate action by the Whig ministry caused the London mob to riot in sympathy with Dr. Sacheverell, which in turn led by a sequence of political events to the downfall of the Whig administration led by Earl Godolphin. Robert Harley, the Tory, assumed the reins of government once more.

Defoe, who had already tasted harsh justice because of his satirical attack on Sacheverell and the High Flyers in *The Shortest Way with the Dissenters* (1702), reached for his pen once more writing a couple of pamphlets—*A Letter from Captain Tom to the Mob* (1710) and *Instructions from Rome in favour of the Pretender* (1710)—which attacked Dr. Sacheverell and other enemies of the established Church. These broadsides together with others in *The Review*[17] on behalf of Godolphin's threatened Whig administration did not prevent Defoe's showing allegiance to Harley's incoming Tory administration in 1710. The moderate Harley found himself head of an administration that was High Flying in character and strong in number. Defoe's *volte-face* provided for his critics a measure of his "trimming" or timeserving.

Defoe's participation in the Sacheverell affair took the form of an attack on one member of Magdalen College, Oxford. But this was not the first time that he had taken upon himself to inveigh against Oxford University on behalf of the established church. In the *Review* of 30th June 1705, he had linked Magdalen College with the church's ruin, no doubt having Dr. Sacheverell in mind from his first brush with that controversial cleric in 1702. It was another cause, however, which led Defoe in 1706[18] to attack the University of Oxford for corrupting future clergy. In doing so he espoused a cause, the battle for which had already been fought and won in 1698 by Jeremy Collier, the non-juring divine, with *A Short View of the Immorality and Profaneness of the English Stage*. Defoe apparently felt he had won a swift victory similar to Collier's, since in 1707, after castigating the University a year before, he congratulated Oxford on banning plays from its precincts.[19] It is problematic as to what extent Defoe influenced this reformation but the student of Defoe can be sure that Defoe had once again acted as the public's conscience in the columns of his *Review* and in doing so had shown himself to be a firm subscriber to the Christian faith.

Howsoever divided the Christian churches might be; howsoever secularly rational some writers, as *philosophes*, might be; or howsoever lax in morals the population as a whole might be, eighteenth-century England was still very much a Christian country. If the epithet 'Augustan' can be applied to a group of writers of Classical persuasion like Pope, Swift, Steele and Addison, the epithet 'Augustinian' can be equally applied to many writers, thinkers and scientists who espoused the Augustinian doctrine of original sin and

24

redemption. Defoe was not alone in his overtly Christian outlook. Writers like Dryden, Cowper, Richardson, Fielding and Steele and clerical writers like Sterne and Swift, all espoused various Christian viewpoints. Great philosophers like John Locke and George Berkeley, Bishop of Cloyne, were clearly Christian thinkers, whilst Isaac Newton and Robert Boyle saw their scientific work as contributing to the greater glory of God. By comparison with these Augustinian thinkers, 'liberal' thinkers were in a minority. Deism, despite its strong associations with the eighteenth-century Enlightenment, was only a minority view.

Education

In view of these facts, it is not surprising that, in the late seventeenth and early eighteenth centuries, the Church still retained its traditional prerogative in education. From time immemorial the Church had been responsible for the education of the young. The Reformation had made little difference to this function since, during Tudor times, the Church became the agent of the State in its newly found interest in education. It became traditional for the Bishop to issue licences to teach. In this way conformity to the Church's teaching and loyalty to the state were achieved. Under James I (James VI of Scotland) the Church continued its hold on education, since the Canons of 1604 upheld the necessity for teachers to hold licences to teach and the taking of an oath continued. Archbishop Laud had been able to enforce a rigid control of education during Charles I's reign by this process of licensing. It was the Act of Uniformity and the rest of the Clarendon Code, passed by the Restoration Parliament, which had sought to restate some of the Canons of 1604 and caused some clergy, schoolmasters and other laity to dissent and break away from the established church. The Act of Uniformity had required all schoolmasters to conform to the liturgy and had threatened imprisonment for those who were not licensed to teach. Some two-thousand Puritan clergy refused to conform to this and were ejected from their livings on St. Bartholomew's day, 24th August 1662. Similarly the Five Mile Act of 1665 made it illegal for such ejected clergy to teach in schools or to come within five miles of any corporate town. In pursuance of this educational policy, the Church seemed more concerned with heresy than with ignorance.

The Church's stranglehold over education was weakened considerably by what has become known by educational legalists and historians as Bates's case. William Bates was a schoolmaster against whom an action was brought, in 1670, for teaching without a bishop's licence. The court decided that since Bates was a nominee of the founder, a lay patron, he could not be ejected from his post by the Bishop. Following this judgment a great many educational endowments were made, some of which helped the cause of Dissenters.

The Cox case in 1700 was equally important and further delimited the power of the Bishops over education in so far as a judgment was given that a licence was not necessary in writing schools, reading schools, dancing schools and other schools of a special nature. This case allowed private individuals to set up schools teaching the rudiments without reference to the Church, which in the eyes of the law-courts was not to be totally responsible for elementary education. The freedom won by these two legal cases was diminished to a certain extent by the Schism Act (1714) to which reference has already been made in connection with Defoe's guardianship of Dissenters' educational interests.[20]

The eighteenth century saw the development in Great Britain of the first organized provision of elementary education. Support of the charity school movement, fully documented by M. G. Jones in her definitive work of that title, was the favourite form of philanthropic contribution. The main impetus in the provision of charity schools came from the Anglican Church which, in 1699, founded the Society for Promoting Christian Knowledge (S.P.C.K.) to promote Anglican Charity Schools.[21] Among the foundation members of this society was Sir Humphrey Mackworth, M.P., with whom Defoe publicly disagreed in a pamphlet entitled *Giving Alms no Charity* (1704). The dispute was about Sir Humphrey's proposals concerning work houses. The charity school movement flourished greatly till about 1729 when the S.P.C.K. began to devote its energies to overseas missions and to printing. Defoe took an interest in the charity schools, although very few were non-conformist schools.

Defoe took an even greater interest in the dissenting academies which, from the 1660's to the beginning of the nineteenth century, flourished in various parts of England but which, unlike the charity schools, formed no organized movement. The educational institutions to which the dissenting academies were alternatives were the endowed grammar schools and the universities. Defoe, himself, has little to say on the endowed grammar schools *per se* but during his lifetime these schools were fairly moribund because of abuses of endowments and the decline in their value. Nor did the continued adherence to a rigidly Classical curriculum help to recruit pupils for these schools. The universities, too, were traditional in character and have been criticized for idleness and inactivity in the eighteenth century by both contemporary and later critics.[22] Considering the recognition by Trevelyan of Defoe as exemplifying the late seventeenth and early eighteenth centuries, it was a glaring oversight on his part not to have recourse to Defoe when dealing with education in that period.

Daniel Defoe and His Times

Having examined, however briefly, the social, political, religious end educational contexts, I need to try to link these contexts with Defoe's life over a period of seventy years. Some cross-referencing is inevitable where episodes in Defoe's life have already been placed in these preceding contexts. Such cross-referencing is not only inevitable but also desirable if the links are to be satisfactorily established.

It is not certain exactly when Defoe was born but it was in either 1660 or 1661, in the parish of St. Gile's, Cripplegate. His mother Alice and father James Foe were a religious couple, who, being loyal members of Dr. Samuel Annesley's Presbyterian congregation, wanted their son Daniel to be a dissenting minister. Daniel Defoe was sent to the private dissenting school of the Rev. Mr. Fisher at Dorking where he received his early education. Defoe, in *An Essay on the History and Reality of Apparitions* (1727), made reference to his early school days at Dorking and was able in his *A Tour thro' the whole island of Great Britain* (1725-27) to show detailed knowledge of this Surrey town. He graduated in about 1674 to a leading dissenting academy at Newington Green run by Dr. Charles Morton, who later emigrated to America and became the first vice-president of Harvard University. This should indicate that the academy gave Defoe a high quality of education. Frequently in his writings he made reference to his education received there and to the enlightened methods of his famous schoolmaster. Because of the breadth of the curriculum and the resulting diminished emphasis on the Classics by Morton, Defoe was less adept with the Classics than would have been gentlemen educated more conventionally in endowed classical grammar schools and universities. His acquaintance, however, with scientific study would recommend his education to those looking with hindsight from the twentieth century. There would be few who received such a scientific and practical education as did the future projector, merchant, tradesman, author and journalist.

Despite his father's career plans, Defoe decided to engage in the commercial and trading world. By the early 1680's he had established himself as a merchant in a prosperous district near the Royal Exchange, and as a wholesale merchant he was captured by Algerian pirates between Harwich and Holland but was quickly released. Already he was acquiring experiences which were to serve as factual bases for his fictional writings. In 1684, he married Mary Tuffley, the daughter of a wine-cooper, who gave him a dowry of £3,700 with his daughter. The facts about Defoe's participation in Monmouth's rebellion the following year are obscure. Several of his former schoolfellows died in the service of this Protestant cause but Defoe, as already mentioned, managed to escape without capture.

The years following Sedgemoor are clouded in mystery since Defoe was no doubt 'lying low' after this debâcle. It is likely, however, that he spent a few years travelling extensively in both Britain and on the continent. Defoe was successively a hose-factor and an importer of wine and tobacco: he also financed merchant shipping and dabbled in insurance. The 1680's were his early trading years which served as a foundation for other enterprises later in real estate, bricks and tiles, oysters, fisheries, linen-weaving and even ship building. From his trading enterprises Defoe learnt much, which is evident in the advice he gives in the two volumes of *The Complete English Tradesman*. He became a liveryman of the City of London in the late 1680's.

As with the precise details of trading activities there are doubts about Defoe's earliest writings. According to John Robert Moore, his earliest publication was in 1683 when Defoe attacked certain Whigs who were supportive of the Turks attacking Vienna. William Lee, on the other hand, the Victorian discoverer of many of Defoe's later works, regarded *A Letter containing some Reflections on His Majesty's Declaration for Liberty of Conscience* (1687) as being his first published work. This was disputed by Leslie Stephen, who in the *Dictionary of National Biography* attributed this pamphlet to Bishop Burnet. In a world of uncertainty about Defoe's publications, it is satisfying to be certain of some aspects of his early years. Nearly all commentators on Defoe noted his presence in the company of horse that escorted the new King and Queen, William and Mary, when they attended the Lord Mayor's banquet at the Guild hall on October 29, 1689. His presence on this ceremonial occasion symbolized his service to these sovereigns and his rising fortunes. By 1690 he was established as an enterprising merchant, with a foot-hold at court, and a reputation of being a wit and man-about-town. During 1690-91, for instance, Defoe wrote for John Dunton's successful periodical, *The Athenian Mercury*. His first major set-back occurred in 1691/ 1692 when he became bankrupt after losing money on shipping, which had been subject to the predations of French privateers; after losing money on a diving-bell project; and after failing to make a profit from the breeding of civet cats for the production of perfume. Defoe did the only thing a potential debtor could do in the seventeenth century. He went into hiding; in his case in Bristol. He had incurred debts amounting to £17,000 but within a few years he had reduced this crippling debt by as much as £12,000. From 1695 to 1699 he was an assistant to Thomas Dalby, one of His Majesty's Commissioners for Glass duties, to whom Defoe dedicated his first major work, *An Essay upon Projects* (1697).

During the 1690's Defoe became a successful pamphleteer, a true son of Grub Street, whom William III employed extensively to publicize his views and policies. William was generous in his rewards to Defoe: and Defoe repaid him in zealous loyalty. As a result of his increasing fortunes, based on his successful political publications, Defoe was able to buy a brick and pantile factory at Tilbury, in Essex. The years between the death of Queen Mary (1694) and the death of William III (1702) were perhaps Defoe's most promising. His ascendant star reached its zenith when in 1701 he had occasion to defend William III and his foreign policy, which involved giving favours to William's Dutch advisers who came to the English court. John Tutchin, another Grub Street hack writer, stirred up traditional English xenophobia with his satirical poem *The Foreigners* to which Defoe replied with *The True-Born Englishman* in January 1701 and won for himself William's continued goodwill. This was perhaps Defoe's finest moment. Such was the success of this poem which set out to explode the myth of national purity that it ran into nine authorized editions as well as several cheap pirated editions, eighty-thousand copies of which were sold for a sixth of the authorized price.

Further, in 1701 he took part in a demonstration involving freeholders from Kent who had petitioned Parliament to declare a pre-emptive war on France which, if it took the initiative, would pose a great threat to the County of Kent. This episode in Defoe's life showed him to be a man of much spirit and courage since the *Legion's Memorial* which he personally presented to the House of Commons supported the Kentish Petition and sought war with France and Spain. In the event of such a war, Defoe had ready a daring scheme for the seizure of Spanish colonies in the West Indies. As already related, the unexpected death of William, who was thrown from his horse after tripping over a mole hill,[23] put Defoe in the cold, in 1702, since it brought about the accession of Queen Anne. Anne declared war on France and Spain with the resultant struggle involving Holland and the Empire in the war of the Spanish Succession. This war of the Spanish Succession lasted from 1702 to 1713 when peace was made at the Treaty of Utrecht.

The accession of Queen Anne in 1702 had been a severe blow to Defoe. Both politically and religiously he was at variance with those High Churchmen and Tories who surrounded the new Queen. At this critical point in his life Defoe had published anonymously *The Shortest Way with the Dissenters*.

His satire, which mischievously poked fun at Anglican High Churchmen, was at first welcomed by most High Churchmen as faithfully reflecting their viewpoint. When it was generally realized, however, that the anonymous writer was none other than the Dissenter Mr. Foe the delight turned to rage. Ironically the Dissenting community also misunderstood Defoe's satirical intentions and showed hostility towards him for his pains.

Defoe was forced to go into hiding to escape the wrath of the High Flyers but he was finally arrested in Spitalfields in 1703. The whole incident was instrumental in passing on to posterity the only surviving description of Defoe, which appeared in the *London Gazette* with an offer of £50 reward for information leading to Defoe's arrest. The *London Gazette* described him as,

> a middle-sized man, about forty years old, of a brown complexion, and dark-brown coloured hair, but wears a wig; a hooked nose, a sharp chin, grey eyes, and a large mole near his mouth. . . .[24]

The Earl of Nottingham, who was responsible for Defoe's arrest, tried to get Defoe to betray Whig secrets, but failed. Defoe was severely punished, being fined, imprisoned and pilloried, after which he was to pay sureties for good behaviour during the next seven years. Meanwhile his *The Shortest Way . . .* was condemned to be burnt, by the common hangman. To be condemned to being placed in the pillory, as was Defoe, was an extremely hard fate, since, being at the mercy of the London mob, the occupant of the pillory could sustain severe physical injury. Defoe was placed in the pillory on three separate days in three separate places and he turned what could have been a nasty situation into one of personal triumph. During his period of imprisonment, before being pilloried, Defoe composed *A hymn to the Pillory*, copies of which he had distributed among the mob who came to mock him. His *Hymn* turned their mockery into open adulation so that instead of being subject to injurious missiles Defoe experienced kisses and garlands. After his experience in the pillory Defoe was detained in Newgate prison. During this time, his brick and pantile business at Tilbury collapsed through enforced neglect, so that once again Defoe's star was in the descendent.

Through the intercession of Robert Harley who had replaced the extremist Tory, Nottingham, Defoe was eventually released but not before the ruin of his business. From the confines of his prison Defoe had begun in 1704 *A Review of the Affairs of France (The Review)* a periodical which was to be published for nine years and, from the end of the first year, published three times a week. This *Review* was managed by Defoe single-handed insofar as he was the sole contributor. For those nine years, through all his busy efforts

30

for the union between England and Scotland, Defoe wrote his thrice-weekly *Review* and even extended his activities by arranging for its publication in Edinburgh as well as in London. This was a most prodigious achievement in journalism. From 1704 Defoe, the Whig Dissenter, became the political agent of Harley, the moderate Tory. His detractors could possibly question how Defoe rationalized his transfer of loyalty to Harley in 1704. Perhaps they shared common ideas of moderation which together with Defoe's pressing penury and Harley's need for a good agent made it a successful partnership. One historian has suggested that Defoe became Harley's Man Friday[25] which, in view of Defoe's relatively humble relationship with Harley compared with Jonathan Swift's relationship with the Tory leader, is an apt description. From 1704 Defoe began his restless career of travelling around Britain on government business and at the same time kept up his political pamphleteering.

While Defoe was engaged in preliminary activities in 1706 for the Union between England and Scotland, he published the important political work *Jure Divino*, a satirical poem about politics, in twelve books consisting of more than three-hundred pages. In the following year the Act of Union was effected, the outcome of which was in no small measure due to the efforts of conciliation by Defoe working for Harley. His *Review* had changed its title in 1707 to *A Review of the State of the English Nation* but in recognition of the Union it was changed yet again in the following year to *A Review of the State of the British Nation*. A change of administration that year, when Godolphin replaced Harley, did not affect unduly Defoe's continuing work as a government agent. He was seemingly as happy with Godolphin as he had been with Harley—at least Godolphin shared Whig sympathies with Defoe. Critics of Defoe might see in this smooth transition yet another case of Defoean opportunism as political 'trimming.' Defoe continued to serve as an intermediary between the two, now politically united, countries. Both in 1708 and 1709 he was once again in Scotland and among the Scots for whom he had a great admiration. In his *Review*[26] he referred to their emphasis on liberal education which compared very favourably with the lack of it among the English gentry. Ever one to make capital out of his experiences, Defoe published in 1709 *The History of the Union of Great Britain* which ran into 694 pages, one of his more copious works. Yet another change of administration in London in 1710, when Robert Harley replaced Godolphin once again, did not affect Defoe's work as a government agent, and this despite the fact that Defoe had, in writing, inveighed against the inflammatory Dr. Henry Sacheverell, who had been instrumental in Godolphin's resignation. Defoe certainly displayed survival qualities second to none but his contemporary, the Vicar of Bray, and even that priority was becoming doubtful.

By 1711, Defoe's fortunes were again in the ascendant. He was by then fully engaged in the political service of Harley (now the Earl of Oxford) and writing several political pamphlets, so that his talents were being used to the full. Nor were financial reward and material comfort denied him. At this time he moved his family to a large residence at Stoke Newington where he was able to keep a house commensurate with the standards of an English gentleman. In 1712, he published *The Present State of Parties in Great Britain*, his major work on the Dissenters in England and Scotland. The closing years of Anne's reign were, however, to be uncertain ones for Defoe. The question of the Hanoverian succession and the ending of the war of the Spanish Succession exercised his mind and pen during these latter years and he was engaged in much political intrigue. He was arrested twice in 1713 for political misdemeanours, only some of which were substantiated, but on both occasions he was released, once on the intercession of the Earl of Oxford. It was in the throes of this kind of political pressure that Defoe ceased publishing his *Review* in 1713. His pen, on the other hand, became more active than ever in the defence of the Dissenters following the Schism Act of 1714 which prevented Dissenters being schoolmasters. In 1714, Defoe published the *Schism Act Explain'd*; *The Weakest go to the Wall*; *A Letter to Mr. Steele*; *A Brief Survey of the Legal Liberties of the Dissenters*; and *The Remedy Worse than the Disease*, all concerned with the defence of the Dissenters. Undoubtedly Defoe had achieved expiation for any wrong Dissenters felt they had sustained from his earlier satire *The Shortest Way with the Dissenters*.

The death of Queen Anne was followed swiftly by the political demise of Viscount Bolingbroke, who had taken over Harley's Tory ministry in the closing days of Anne's reign, and the period which Basil Williams has called the 'Whig Supremacy,' from 1714 to 1760, began. Once again Defoe had been caught backing the wrong horse and to make matters worse he was arrested for the third time in two years for political slander on the Earl of Anglesey. This time there was no Harley to bail him out. Defoe was tried for slander and convicted, but not sentenced; yet his world was, once again, completely shattered. Until the discoveries by William Lee in 1869 of Defoe's journalistic activities, it had been assumed by commentators on Defoe that he had retired from political life to pursue a more quiet and literary career. In fact, Defoe was able to come to a secret arrangement with the new Whig administration whereby his sentence for slander on Anglesey was waived: he was to be released and to engage in Tory journalism but for the sole purpose of diluting or emasculating the Tory periodical press. This was at a time when Jacobitism posed a threat to the continuation of the Hanoverian succession. Once more Defoe changed his political allegiance but this time he was insidiously pretending to be a continuing Tory sympathizer. Defoe kept up this deceit for fifteen years overtly being a Tory supporter among Tory friends but secretly being a Whig agent.

In extant correspondence with Charles De La Faye, secretary to Lord Townsend, the Whig Secretary of State,[27] the secret compact is set out: part of this plan was for Defoe to edit an emasculated Tory periodical called *Mercurius Politicus*, which he did from 1716 to 1720.

Meanwhile the year 1715 may have been a year of immense Jacobite activity; it was also a busy one for Defoe. During the year he published some fifteen works including *The Appeal to Honour and Justice*, which set out to justify his ability for political accommodation and *The Family Instructor*, his first didactic work. Commentators[28] have often regarded this major work by Defoe as a token of expiation for the worldly life he had led. On the other hand it has been suggested[29] that it was probably Defoe's fears expressed in his pamphlet *The Schism Act Explain'd* (1714) that led him to write *The Family Instructor* as a guide and inspiration to Dissenting families who were faced with the problem of family education by this Act. It is likely that both are right since the two motives are complementary rather than mutually exclusive.

During the next five years Defoe sought anonymity while engaged in political intrigue. He became the editor of, or contributor to, several periodicals in addition to the *Mercurius Politicus*. From 1716 to 1718 he contributed to *Dormer's News Letter*, a journal read by the Anglican high church party. From 1716 to 1720 he became a principal contributor, and sometimes editor, of the Jacobite *Weekly Journal* or *Saturday's Evening Post*, generally called *Mist's Weekly-Journal* after Nathaniel Mist, the Jacobite proprietor. On more than one occasion Defoe was able to utilize his secret Whig connections to extricate Mist from trouble incurred by his Jacobitism. For just over a year, from 1718 to 1719, Defoe edited the *Mercurius Britannicus* under the pseudonym of Walter Campbell. In September 1718 he began *The Whitehall Evening Post*, a tri-weekly journal, which venture lasted for two years, till about October 1720. *The Daily Post*, which he began in October 1719 had a longer run lasting till April 1725. He began contributing also, in June 1720, to *The Original Weekly Journal*, usually called *Applebee's Journal*, his connection with which was still very strong in 1726.

Such a journalistic record alone for a man now approaching old age would be extraordinary but when this journalism is linked with his other writings his performance can only be regarded as phenomenal. In 1718 Defoe published the second volume of *The Family Instructor*, the first volume of which had been so popular that it necessitated a second edition within six months. In this year he wrote also *Memoirs of the Life and Eminent Conduct of that Learned and Reverend Divine, Daniel Williams D.D.* and *A Vindication of the Press.* From then on Defoe was less concerned with political issues than with educational and social ones. This was also the beginning of his novel writing period, at the time when he was approaching sixty. The coincidence of these two trends in Defoe's current writings could possibly account for the interest which Defoe showed in his novels to the effects of education. This interest is very evident in both *Moll Flanders* and *Roxana*, but more especially in *Colonel Jacque.* In 1719 he published *Robinson Crusoe* in two parts and it was instantly popular. In the same year Defoe became involved in the quasi-political affair of the charity school sermons for St. Anne's Charity School, Aldersgate, and published in their defence *Charity Still a Christian Virtue.* Varied publications followed in 1720 including *Captain Singleton, Serious Reflections of Robinson Crusoe, The History of the Life and Adventures of Mr. Duncan Campbell (?)*[30] and the *Memoirs of a Cavalier.* Although he was now in his sixties, Defoe's output of publications did not diminish. In 1722 he published *Moll Flanders, Colonel Jacque, Religious Courtship* and *A Journal of the Plague Year,* a work which took him, through the aid of his uncle's reminiscences and contemporary records, back to his childhood days. After a fallow year as far as publications were concerned Defoe produced another bountiful harvest in 1724 when he published *The Fortunate Mistress* or *Roxana, The Great Law of Subordination Consider'd, A Tour thro' the Whole Island of Great Britain,* Vol. 1, *The History of the Remarkable Life of John Sheppard* and the *Robberies and Escapes of John Sheppard.*

In this *annus mirabilis* of publications, Defoe met Henry Baker, the celebrated teacher of the deaf and dumb, who was to become his son-in-law. Defoe had already shown an interest in this area of 'special education' by his *A History...of Duncan Campbell* (1720) and therefore, no doubt, welcomed Baker's attentions to his daughter, Sophia, whom Baker married in 1729.

Defoe's last years were marked by a plethora of publications, some fictional, some biographical and some educational in character. These included, in 1725, *Everybody's Business is Nobody's Business,* an attack on the insolence of servants; *The Tour thro' the Whole Island of Great Britain,* Vol. 2; *Jonathan Wild,* a biography on the organizer of London thieves in the early eighteenth century; and, more importantly, *The Compleat English Trades-*

man, Vol. 1. The following year, 1726, saw the publication of *The Tour,* Vol. 3; *Mere Nature Delineated,* an examination of Peter the Wild Boy; *An Essay upon Literature; A General History of the Principal Discoveries and Improvements in the Useful Arts;* and, more importantly, *The Protestant Monastery,* which was an attack on the ingratitude of youth.

The first year of George II's reign, 1727, was important educationally insofar as two didactic volumes, *The Complete English Tradesman,* Vol. II and *The New Family Instructor,* were published. There is a certain cyclical nature in Defoe's educational writings. His first educational ideas were expressed in *An Essay upon Projects* when he advocated the education of women and his last published work dealing with education—*Augusta Triumphans,* published in 1728—is also a series of projects. His public recognition as a man of letters had come to him *via* a book on projects; it was therefore fitting that his very last published works should be of this character, even though such projects were concerned with preventing robberies rather than making capital.

Defoe's final years were dogged by failing health and persistent creditors who finally forced him to go into hiding. In this way Defoe finished his days in obscurity dying 'of a lethargy' in Ropemaker's Alley, London, on 24th April 1731. He was buried in the Dissenters' cemetery at Bunhill Fields two days later, launched on what he once described as "the great ocean of eternity."

CHAPTER 3

Defoe: The Critic of Education

Defoe's basic attitude towards the ability to educate was both genetic and environmental: it was genetic insofar as he believed that no amount of education could make a silk purse out of a sow's ear; it was environmental insofar as he believed that mere Nature alone was insufficient in the battle of life. Education was necessary: the clay of nature needed to be moulded on the wheel of nurture. These two discrete viewpoints were cogently expressed by Defoe in two separate works. In *The Present State of the Parties in Great Britain* (1712), where he was discussing the recruitment of boys for the Dissenting ministry, he wrote:

> If the Boy be a Clod, a meer Stupid, a Block without a Head or if he be a Flutter, a meer Feather, the one too hard, the other too soft; one too thick, and the other too thin for a Stock of learning; one so contracted in the Head there is no room to hold it, the other so thin there's no Power to retain it, to what Purpose should Schoolmasters go to invert Nature, and force the Current? Give a Blockhead Learning; you make him a worse kind of Blockhead than he was before.[1]

Defoe complemented this sentiment fourteen years later when, in his *Mere Nature Delineated* (1726), he referred with approval to an inscription which he recalled written above the door of a free-school in Somersetshire[2] which read as follows:

> When education does adorn
> The Minds of Children nobly born,
> They seem of an Angelick Race,
> But where good education wants
> To be engrafted in young plants
> It renders them extremely base.[3]

It is quite likely that Defoe composed the rhyme and that his concrete reference to a school in Somerset combined with the verse was yet another example of his gaining verisimilitude by mixing fact with fiction. Whatever is the case, it does not alter the fact of Defoe's belief in the need for education: and even if he would not go along with later writers on education like Helvétius for whom 'L'education peut tout,' at least, in his writings, he appears as a firm advocate of it.

Defoe's advocacy of education is perhaps no more strongly in evidence than when he is considering the education of women. For this reason he criticizes the contemporary practice of providing women with no more than polite accomplishments. From the pages of *An Essay upon Projects* (1697), Defoe's condemnation of the contemporary treatment of women by failing to provide them with equal educational opportunity rings out loud and clear. He wrote:

> I have often thought of it as one of the most barbarous Customs in the world, considering us as a Civiliz'd and a Christian Countrey, that we deny the advantages of Learning to Women. We reproach the Sex every-day with Folly and Impertinence, while I am confident, had they the advantages of Education equal to us, they wou'd be guilty of less than ourselves.[4]

Defoe felt strongly that to teach girls to read and embroider only was to leave them virtually in a state of mere Nature. Defoe therefore proposed amongst his early projects an academy for women. Closer consideration of this project will be given in Chapter 5, suffice it to affirm at this stage Defoe's criticism of existing education for women. As he averred in his *Review* "We always thought the Women had the quickest and justest Notions of things at first sight, *tho' we have unjustly rob'd them of the Judgment, by denying them early Instruction*" (Defoe's italics).[5]

The Universities and Endowed Schools

Some of Defoe's strongest educational criticism was levelled at the Universities of Oxford and Cambridge. Oxford was especially criticized not so much for its lack of learning as for its immorality in allowing plays to be put on without due regard for propriety; and, for yet another reason, Magdalen College, Oxford, was subject to Defoe's additional censure because, as previously noted, Magdalen was the College of which the notorious Dr. Henry Sacheverell was a Fellow.[6]

Much of Defoe's criticism of Oxford is to be found in the pages of his *Review*. His criticism is perhaps less effective than criticism of Oxford to be found in the pages of another periodical of similar title, published in Edinburgh in the nineteenth century. That criticism contributed substantially to the ground-swell which led to the Royal Commissions of enquiry into the universities in the 1850's: Defoe's criticism made no such impact, although Defoe himself no doubt felt justified in his criticism and its outcome.

As a Puritan who was excluded from the universities because of his religion, Defoe was highly critical of the seemingly debauched university of Oxford where plays were sometimes held. He wrote, in the *Review* on 8th August 1706,

> That our two great and famous Universities are allow'd to be exemplar in their Learning, Antiquities, Libraries and Rarities, and remarkable for the Number and Capacities of the Men of Letters now among them, I readily allow; what a pity it is then, that they should not equally flourish in Vertue, and how mad they must be, that would sacrifize the Reputation of their whole Body to the Pleasures and Follies of an Interlude![7]

Paradoxically enough, Defoe the Dissenter, was concerned for the morals of future Anglican clergymen being educated at the university; their virtue was being insidiously assaulted he felt by the irreverence and bawdiness to be found in contemporary plays. He cautioned College Heads in the same article with:

> Pray, Gentlemen, reflect upon the Care of Youth under your Hands, and what sober Parents will ever commit their Sons to your charge?[8]

And again:

> For God's sake, Gentlemen, look back upon the Gift of your pious Founders, who built, and so plentifully endow'd the several Colleges and Houses that form your University. How do the Preambles of their Gifts frequently introduce the Bounty with these words, 'For the Honour of God, encouragement of Learning, the Encrease of Vertue Piety, and true Religion, I give and grant etc.'[9]

In another *Review* article two days later Defoe is more explicit when he refers to "the loose and lewd Excursions of our Mob Wit, and common Street Eloquence" which "crowd the young ears of those, who are sent there to be initiated into a Love of Learning and Vertue."[10] Jeremy Collier, the national scourge of risqué theatre at the end of the seventeenth century, could not have been more explicit in condemnation. Defoe was writing on behalf of the nation since, he argued, it was necessary for the health of the nation that the sons of its leading families be reared properly in virtue. He found particularly objectionable the practice in the theatre of depicting clergymen as objects of fun being "made the Sport of the Stage" since this was inculcating in the young an irreverence for the holy office. How could future clergy take their vocation seriously if it were an object of fun? Such censure would seem heavy criticism even in the moralistic Victorian age.

In his censure of Oxford, Defoe advised his readers that Cambridge was a better place since "Cambridge is by far the best governed University" and

"there is no *Play-house* allow'd there." A year later, however, his readers noted through correspondence to the editor, Mr. Review (Defoe), that Oxford University had expelled its theatre players. The letter (most likely written by Defoe) concluded by thanking him for contributing to this reformation.[11]

Defoe's most concentrated criticism on universities is to be found in his *Reasons for a Royal Visitation* (1717), a lengthy pamphlet of some sixty-four pages. In it he states unequivocally that *"in order to furnish the Church of England with a Succession of Pious, Learned, and Laborious Ministers, it is absolutely necessary to Reform our Universities"* (Defoe's italics). He accused the clergy graduating from the universities (Cambridge was included in this censure) of being ignorant, and blamed their tutors for conniving at unscholarly pursuits at the University. Where Defoe breaks new ground in his criticism of educational institutions is in his condemnation of the endowed public schools[12] for being the seed-beds of disaffection for the universities. Westminster, Eton, Canterbury and Winchester are mentioned by name as being responsible for this early "tainting" of youth. The extent of this criticism is a little surprising since the eighteenth-century endowed schools, no doubt deserving of criticism and being partly rivals to Dissenting Academies, were not subjected to any sustained attack or criticism by Defoe. Rather the reverse was the case. In *The Compleat English Gentleman* (1729) he praised the schools of Eton, Winchester, Westminster, Felsted, Bishop Stortford, Canterbury and others for educating the sons of "some of the best families in England" ... "with great success."[13]

The Charity Schools

The Charity Schools, largely Anglican institutions, are also not subjected to much of Defoe's criticism. Encomium rather than censure is given them for their most worthy educational objective of helping the poor in the education of their young. There was one occasion, however, when Defoe was critical of those responsible for organizing and financing charity schools. His criticism is of value to the historian of education insofar as it is a contemporary comment on the decline of effort in the charity school movement. M. G. Jones suggests in *The Charity School Movement* that the S.P.C.K.'s interest began to wane in about 1729 partly because of its alternative interests in overseas missions and publishing. Defoe, writing in the *Applebee Journal*, as early as 19th November 1720, commented on the continuing efforts of the Oxford Society in London (not mentioned by Miss Jones) for educating poor children when other societies had gone out of existence. According to Defoe the early supporters of the Charity Schools "talk'd too much, and did too little." Defoe is redolent of Bernard Mandeville when he writes:

> How comes it to pass, that we hear no more of them? That their great Cavalcades thro' the City of *London* are forgot, their Colours and Streamers laid aside, the poor Orphans pretended to be taken into their Care, neglected, disabled from setting up the Trades they were put out to, and so left in a worse Case than they were found?[14]

It would seem that some years before 1729, the charity school movement was already in decline.

Dissenting Academies

Since Defoe was a Dissenter, proud of his education at Dr. Morton's dissenting academy, it is surprising to find Defoe also critical of some aspects of Dissenting education. His strictures on dissenting academies are to be found in *The Present State of the Parties in Great Britain* (1712), perhaps one of Defoe's less readable major works. In it he criticized the lack of discrimination by dissenting academies in recruiting their pupils, who were largely destined for the Dissenting ministry. The practice was criticized whereby boys from poor families, who were unsuited for other modes of employment because of physical or other handicaps, were given financial assistance to attend a dissenting academy. In such cases Defoe complained that there "is not a Word of Enquiry made into the Genius, the Capacity, or the Inclination of the Child, or Children. The Case *is not* what they are fit for, but they must not be Starved; the poor Woman must be reliev'd, perhaps the Boy is a Native Blockhead."[15] "It were much better," wrote Defoe that, "they were made *Porters, Grooms,* or any lawful Mechanick; that way they might get their Livings; but the other is to breed them up as if on purpose to be dispis'd Beggars, and Starve."[16] In a letter to Robert Harley of 21st May 1714 Defoe had alluded to the "beggars and drones" who had been "bred up for Ministers" at the dissenting academies.[17]

Defoe was critical, too, of the brevity of the education received by those who were financed on Charity funding. Because it was necessary for the butter to be spread as thinly as possible in order that as many as possible could benefit from this funding, those going through the dissenting academies under these arrangements were given an attenuated education. Many dissenting ministers were being turned out of the academies therefore inadequately prepared for their vocation, and their education compared unfavourably with the scholarship and erudition of the early dissenting ministers.

Defoe felt, in line with the Moderns, that those academies which persisted in spending time on the classics to the neglect of English were in error. (He would be very aware of the controversy between the Ancients and Moderns which educationally could be seen to be reflected in the gradual replacement of Classical Studies by studies in the vernacular.) In Defoe's view, the time invested in the study of the Classics was incommensurate with the benefits derived from it. He was convinced, too, that the universities had an advantage over the academies insofar as there was greater scope at the university for social intercourse, which observation was educationally percipient on Defoe's part. He wrote:

> 'Tis evident, the great Imperfection of our Accademies is want of Conversation; this the Publick Universities enjoy; ours cannot.[18]

Of the dissenting academies Defoe wrote:

> from our Schools we have abundance of Instances of Men that come away Masters of Science, Cricticks in the *Greek* and *Hebrew*, perfect in Languages; and perfectly Ignorant (if that Term may be allow'd) of their Mother Tongue, especially as to the Beauties of Stile, Cadence, and Politeness of Language.[19]

Defoe adopted a Quintilianesque position in his advocacy of verbal fluency amongst future dissenting ministers when he wrote:

> It is true, the Head is the main Thing that a Tutor is to see Furnish'd; but the Tongue must be Tuned, or he'll make no Musick with the voice. ... Acceptable Words, a good Diction, a Grave, yet Polite, and easie stile in the *English*, is a most taking and valuable Thing in a Minister, and without which his Learning cannot exert itself: This we find generally neglected, and left wholly to Nature.[20]

Defoe made some constructive suggestions about how the fault could be remedied but these will be examined in the next chapter.

The Lack of Education Among the Gentry

Defoe's most forthright and trenchant criticism is reserved, however, for the lack of education among the English gentry. Not being regarded by the English gentry as a gentleman himself because of his 'commercial' and dissenting background, Defoe found much to criticize in the gentry. No doubt his analysis of what constituted 'gentlemen' and his scathing comments about their lack of learning were conditioned, to a certain extent, by his being regarded as less than a gentleman himself. This motivated him possibly to revert to a sentiment expressed strongly in *The True-Born Englishman* that all so-called 'gentlemen' have relatively humble beginnings. Just as it was

41

possible for all true-born Englishmen to be found 'foreign' in origins if the family tree were to be traced back far enough, so likewise gentility, if traced back a few generations is generally to be found to have humble origins. Defoe wrote:

> They that look farthest back must lose their Fathers in the Search, or they will lose themselves as to the thing they search for; they must stop *some where*, or they will find themselves *no where*; they must run at last into a Beginning that will baulk the Enquiry, and bring them all to nothing, that is to the *Cannaille* and to the *mob*. (Defoe's italics)[21]

He waxed satirical on contemporary snobbery in society when he observed that

> In *England* we desire no greater honour than to say our line can be trac'd back to the Conqueror, and that our ancestor came over with the conqueror:
>
> > *Tho' what the hero was no man can tell,*
> > *Whether a Drummer or a Colonell.*[22]

Such gentle satire was mild, however, compared with Defoe's comments on the ignorance of the gentry. This ignorance, characteristic of many of the gentry was complemented by boorishness, drunkenness and a wastrel existence. But he was by no means the only critic of the English gentry in the eighteenth century. William Darrell, it is thought, wrote *The Gentleman Instructed* (1704) in which he observed of the gentry that

> Their Study is to learn sins; their employment to commit 'em, and grand Diversion to applaud their Impieties.[23]

Similarly Bishop Thomas Wilson in a sermon preached on 28th May 1724 and published in *The True Christian Method of Educating Children* (1787) referred to the gentry's behaviour as "the vile Ingratitude of living only to dishonour their great Benefactor."[24] Both of these writers, however, were sanctimonious in their attitudes to the gentry. True, Defoe also could be sanctimonious in his observations as any reader of *The Family Instructor* will attest, but whereas William Darrell (1651-1721) was a Jesuit who was long domiciled on the continent, whose chief works were theological or religiously polemicist in character; and Thomas Wilson (1663-1755) was Bishop of Sodor and Man from 1697, and was responsible for drawing up, in 1707, 'Ecclesiastical Constitutions' for restoration of discipline in church, Defoe was, by comparison, a man of the world. Observations on the English gentry from Liège and the Isle of Man were likely to be less well grounded than those of one who travelled constantly through the length and breadth of England.

Defoe was prone to repetition in his writing especially where he wished to hammer home a point. Ignorance among the English gentry was a theme which he repeated often in *The Compleat English Gentleman* so that condemnation of this ignorance abounds. At a relatively early stage in the work, he wrote:

> For here our gentlemen are brought up in the most obstinate ignorance and folly, and fill'd early with the most riveted aversions to learning and improvement in the very face of an improving and knowing age, in spite of the encouragement every-where given to polite learning; where arts and science flourish before their faces, and when the age they live in and the country they live in is particularly fam'd over the whole Christian world for the highest improvements in the sublimest studyes....[25]

Defoe then went on to link this ignorance with other complementary aspects of the English gentry denounced by William Darrell, Bishop Wilson and others. He wrote:

> But I am told, even while I am writing these sheets, that if I expect to make any impression upon the age in this way of arguing I must change my method; that to talk to the gentlemen, of learning and improvement, after they have tasted the sweets of idleness and pleasure is to talk gospell to a kettle-drum; that after they have follow'd the dogs and hawks, and eas'd their Fateagues of the chase with the bottle, there is no room for instruccion; but they go on, then, by the impetuosity of their own gust, following one game with another till the habit is rooted, till the blockhead and the heir are blended together and become inseperable; that then the ignorance is seated in the blood as well as in the brain, and the brute becomes naturall to the man....[26]

Much later in *The Compleat English Gentleman* he scornfully dismisses the gentry with the succinct observation that,

> *They're born, they live, they laugh, they know not why; They sleep, eat, drink, get heirs, grow fat, and dye.* (Defoe's italics)

Defoe is, of course, rather sweeping in his condemnation since despite his own analysis at the beginning of *The Compleat English Gentleman* that there are two types of gentlemen, namely the born gentleman and the bred gentleman, he does not distinguish, in his condemnation, between the different types. His remarks seem to be pertinent only to the 'time wasting, pleasure seeking' country squire, the Squire Western of Fielding's *Tom Jones*, whose main concerns are hunting and hawking. Again, Defoe's gentleman is not unlike Oliver Goldsmith's Tony Lumpkin, who is epitomised as the country bumpkin unable to read. As Defoe declared:

> 'Tis a scandalous thing enough to see gentlemen of fortunes and families, and who value themselves upon their birth, quallity, and estates, that can hardly write their own names, at least that can't write legibly, suppose they had a letter to write upon the most extraordinary occasion.[28]

In his condemnatory criticism of the English gentry, therefore, Defoe lumps together the ignorant majority making no distinctions between them, while acknowledging the bright few among the gentry as being some of the more intelligent leaders of the nation. He suggested that "the great defect lyes not in their families or in their blood, not in their intellect or capascities, but in the error of their education."[29] This 'error of their education' lay in a neglect of liberal education; in the inculcation of a love of pleasure instead of a love of learning, which in turn is an obstacle to a love of virtue. Defoe acknowledged that men can learn to be fools as well as be wise and that the employment of private tutors is often the reason for this turning to folly. Often tutors are at the mercy of the whims of the growing youth who have to be placated if the tutor is to retain his post. In his condemnation of the private tutor, therefore, Defoe took the opposite view from that of John Locke and Jean Jacques Rousseau both of whom envisaged education taking place through the medium of a tutor.

Summary

In sum, Defoe was a critic of some aspects of contemporary education. The higher up the social scale the pupil, the greater was Defoe's criticism. He was strongly critical, therefore, of education of the gentry; aware of possible abuses in the education of the Dissenters of the middling ranks and least critical of the education of the poor. The criticism was the criticism of an advocate of education and it is this facet of Defoe's educational thought which I now examine in chapter 4.

Defoe: The Advocate of Education

The Education of the Gentleman

Despite its being a vehicle of Defoe's criticism, *The Compleat English Gentleman* did have a constructive purpose which was to advise the ignorant gentry how they could cut their losses and acquire a liberal education in a relatively short time. Defoe saw his first task as eradicating the gentry's scorn for learning which they denounced as pedantry. He posed the question:

> How shall we perswade those gentlemen not to bring their sons up in the same ignorance, which they think is so far from being a scandal, that 'tis the ornament of a gentleman? How shall we prevail with them to giv their eldest sons any learning, while they think 'tis below their quallity?[1]

The answer to this question is to be found in Defoe's concept of 'Post entries' or, in modern parlance, Adult Education. If there could be a generation of gentlemen who had experienced a liberal education then it would be possible to perpetuate this happy state since this cultural heritage would be transmitted to the next generation: the vicious cycle of the uneducated bequeathing ignorance to their young would be broken. Defoe saw the solution in giving, to the gentry, a second chance for education. He wrote

> Tho' [they] were not made schollars when [they] were boys, [they] need not go block-heads to the grave. Is there nothing to be learnt now, because [they] learn't nothing then?[2]

Defoe's solution was autodidactism: the gentlemen seeking an education late in life should teach themselves. According to Defoe,

> Our gentry are not what we call born fools ... They have generally naturall powers, but the grand difficiency is want of erudition, want of teaching. .... There are methods of instruccion to be found out which are neither below the quallity of a gentleman to make use of, or unsuitable to his yeares ... and yet I am not for sending them to school in their adult state, and putting gentlemen at 30 or 40 years of age to learn their accidence. ... They shall be their own perceptors, their own tutors, and themselves shall instruct themselves.[3]

Defoe perceived, as many have perceived since, that the adult has several maturational advantages over the child in the process of learning. To begin with, motivation in the adult is much stronger since it springs from a will to learn rather than from the goadings of pedagogy. Defoe observed of adult learners,

> such voluntary students, such gentlemen, who thus being sencible of the deficiency of their educacion have applyed themselves by a voluntary study to recover the loss, make a swifter progression by many degrees than those who are taught young and under the discipline of paedogogues and domineering masters, who think to drive Greek and Latin into them with a beetle and wedges, as men clear blocks, and who, in a word, spoil as many scholars as they make.[4]

Another advantage which the adult has over the youth in the process of learning is that he does not have to rely on memory. Where mature understanding is undeveloped the task of Memory (to adopt discarded faculty psychology terminology) is increased by way of compensation. With the adult, mature reasoning is brought to bear on the process of learning and is not a compensatory device. Defoe suggested that reason would thus facilitate the studies of those who take up learning late.[5]

Defoe suggested various ways in which the 'post entry' could proceed with the least difficulty, since he would be without either Latin or Greek, the twin bases of traditional learning. Translations of Classical works were advocated which, according to Defoe, would give the 'post entry' the fruits of scholarship with much less sweat. He asked

> Is it worth any gentleman's while . . . to go seaven year to Grammar Bridewell (the school) and there beat Greek and Latin, as whores beat hemp? Is it worth all this labour to make a man able to read and compare the originals, when he can read and may depend upon the justice of the translation?[6]

Complementary to this suggestion was that of the universities' adopting the vernacular as the medium of instruction for all studies. Drawing upon his own experience at Dr. Morton's dissenting academy, Defoe suggested that all studies might, with profit, be conducted in English.[7] Yet another suggestion which emanated from his Stoke Newington schooldays was the adoption of a wide curriculum by his 'post entries.' The use of the globes and the knowledge of maps, in other words Geography, could be studied in English and would be a useful adjunct to their studies. Science, too, he thought could be studied profitably by the many through the vernacular. Defoe declared:

> confining these most necessary branches of science to those onely who can read and understand Latin is tying up knowledge to a few, whereas Science being a publick blessing to mankind ought to be extended and made

as difusiv as possible, and should, as the Scripture sayes of sacred knowledge, spread over the whole earth, as the waters cover the sea.[8]

Defoe, it would seem, wanted to take Shamanism out of education.

English, Language and Literature, was another useful area of study in a widened curriculum since as Defoe observed,

> many gentlemen come from the University excellently well skilled in the sciences, Masters, nay critics, in the oriental languages and in most parts of usefull learning and can hardly spell their mother tongue.[9]

Defoe was casting stones from a very vulnerable glass-house since his own orthography was itself somewhat idiosyncratic. Complementary to his suggestion for the study of English in a widened curriculum which would include also History, Mathematics and Astronomy, was his devaluation of the study of Latin as a subject. Like Locke before him, Defoe emphasized the utility somewhat illogically for a treatise on the education of a gentleman,

> if Latin and Greek was necessary to a study of Astronomy, Navigation, and, in generall, several other branches of the Mathematicks, what would become of Navigation in generall; for where is there a sea-faring man in twenty that understands Latin, and yet some of them the compleatest artists in the world.[10]

His main point, however, is clear: it is that Latin is not vital in the real world of which the gentleman was a part. Defoe, therefore, was very encouraging to gentlemen without learning. Through his suggestions for self-education Defoe felt that,

> no gentlemen ought to throw up the point and grow desperate because he was not sent to school, as he ought to have been, in his childhood, and been made master of the learned languages in the time of it, seeing it is never too late; ...

According to Defoe

> he may still form his genius with the sublimest studyes, and store himself with all the learning necessary to make him a complete gentleman.[11]

The Education of the Tradesman

Though Defoe offered sound advice on the education of a gentleman, the background from which he drew for his gentlemanly advice, was shaky. Rather like Defoe, the novelist, when writing *Roxana, or the Fortunate Mistress*, he was not in full control of his subject material. He was not completely *au courant* with Roxana's aristocratic world neither was he emphatic in his consideration of the gentleman since he was not one of them. This could not be said of Defoe's advice on the education of a tradesman, for he had both tasted the fruits of success and learnt the lessons of adversity in several trading enterprises both in England and abroad. He was in fact a man of the world, and, as he suggests in his *The Compleat English Tradesman*, Vol. I, "knowledge of the world . . . is the best education." His two volumes on *The Compleat English Tradesman*, in fact, epitomize Defoe's belief in the superiority of experience over study and in doing so form a treatise on eighteenth-century business methods. At the same time they epitomize 'pragmatic' principles. In volume one Defoe examined thoroughly the skills involved in bookkeeping and letter writing. His advice was full of common sense about letter writing:

> a tradesman's letters should be plain, concise, and to the purpose; no quaint expressions, no book-phrases, no flourishes and yet they must be full and sufficient to express what he means, so as not to be doubtful, much less unintelligible.[12]

Simplicity and plainness of style were stressed by Defoe as being necessary in writing on all subjects. Similarly, he averred,

> The end of speech is that men might understand one another's meaning; certainly that speech, or that way of speaking which is most easily understood, is the best way of speaking.[13]

Defoe was mindful of the need for clear communication between individuals as is evidenced in his emphasis on plainness and simplicity of style, but his advice on communication went beyond generalities to specifics. He advised, for instance, on the need for tradesmen to learn the technical terminology of each other's trades, thereby facilitating communication and creating business confidence. This did not mean that the tradesman had to learn every trade although, according to Defoe, "he should have a true notion of business in general, and a knowledge how and in what manner it is carried on"; further "he should know where every manufacture is made, and how bought at first hand; [and] he should know which are the proper markets, and what the particular kinds of goods to exchange at those markets."[14] In his advice to others, Defoe was, of course, reflecting his own universal skill and knowledge, built up over a period of forty years.

In the second volume of *The Complete English Tradesman*, published two years later in 1727, Defoe considered the qualities to be sought in a good tradesman. It is not without significance that he regarded the need for knowing one's station as of prime importance. As one who gave up a possible life of scholarship and Christian ministering for trade, Defoe was in a good position to observe that the person who bemoaned a commercial station in life, and would rather have attended university, was a lost soul. Applying the law of subordination to an intellectual scale, Defoe advised that a tradesman should aim for a *via media* between being a scholar and a dunce. No doubt bearing in mind his own early experiences, Defoe ridiculed academic pretensions in tradesmen. He wrote:

> A Wit, turn'd Tradesman! What an incongruous Part of Nature is there brought together, consisting of direct contraries? No apron Strings will hold him; 'tis in vain to lock him in behind the Compter, he's gone in a *Moment*; instead of Journal and Ledger, he runs away to his Virgil and Horace; his Journal entries are all Pindaricks and his Ledger is all Heroicks.[15]

Brian Fitzgerald has likened Defoe to H. G. Wells: the two men had much in common. Both had links with trade, since Wells' father owned a draper's shop in Bromley; both resisted parental pressures in their choice of a career; both entered literature via journalism and used their literature as a vehicle of expression of social views; both wrote romance of either tall ships or spaceships; and both formulated projects of social reconstruction.[16] It is the last mentioned comparison about the formulation of projects, to which W. H. G. Armytage also alludes when he calls Defoe "the eighteenth century H. G. Wells."[17] This is the aspect of Defoe which is to be examined next.

Defoe the Educational Projector

As a leading projector in an age of Projects in which men responded to the challenge of maritime exploration and scientific discovery, Defoe's mind was actively engaged with projects for the improvement of mankind. In one of his last works, for instance, *The Generous Projector* (1731) he put forward proposals *inter alia* for a foundling hospital for illegitimate children; for the prevention of women being put away by their husbands into madhouses and for the prevention of daily abuses by Watermen. Much of this late work was contained verbatim earlier in *Augusta Triumphans* (1728) which set out for consideration several projects for the improvement of education.

Perhaps the most important of Defoe's projects in education was, anticipating the Utilitarians in the nineteenth century, his proposal for the institution of a university at London. A third university at Durham, to complement Oxford and Cambridge and to compete in number with Scottish universities, had been proposed during the Cromwellian interregnum, but the proposal had come to naught. Nor was his proposal for a university in London original and as he readily recognized in *Augusta Triumphans,* Gresham College provided a proto-type of this kind of metropolitan institution. His strictures on Oxford and Cambridge have been considered already in Chapter 3. In *Reasons for a Royal Visitation,* his desire for the reform of the universities, which had been the subject of his criticism in the *Review,* was sufficiently strong for him to think of a university education beyond Oxford and even Cambridge. He noted that many of the gentry sent their sons to be educated abroad "for fear of their being ruin'd, instead of instructed, at our Universities."[18] His proposal for a university in London was, therefore, a natural extension of his reflections upon Oxford and Cambridge. Reasons for a university in the capital were strong: (i) potential students would be saved from a wastrel life since many would not be far from the influence of their families; (ii) there would be a great saving in family expenses; and (iii) it would add to the reputation of London itself which would become a "scene of science."

In his concrete proposal for the University of London, Defoe showed the talent of the visionary when he referred to its proposed collegiate base. It was one thing to have a collegiate-based University at Oxford or Cambridge; it was quite another to envisage such in the nation's capital. Defoe envisaged that the students would live at home but that they would dine in college. College would be a place for providing separate study rooms and for lodging their books "for 'twould be most inconvenient to lug them backwards and forwards."[19] Defoe's proposals were in one other way, extraordinary. He proposed the use of the endowed schools in and near London such as Westminster, Eton, Charterhouse, St. Paul's and Merchant Taylors', as "Colleges for University Education ... where Youth might begin and end their Studies."[20] This proposal was, of course, killing two birds with one stone, since in *Reasons for a Royal Visitation* Defoe had blamed the schools as being seedbeds of disaffection. By being linked to the new university, thus receiving a new function, the schools themselves would be transformed and Oxford and Cambridge would become more amenable to reform.

In *Augusta Triumphans,* Defoe also put forward proposals to improve Music and Music Education. Confessing to having been a lover of music since boyhood and no mean performer on the Viol and Lute, he recommended Music as "a most genteel and commendable accomplishment." Having noted the English support of Italian opera, Defoe proposed an Academy which would train English musicians, especially vocalists. His plans entailed the formation of an academy of Music on the foundation of Christ's Hospital School. Thirty boys were to be selected to form an élite body of singers who would, in addition, be divided into three instrumentalist Classes with three Music masters. Girls were to be included if sufficiently gifted.

His proposed time-table for this Music academy, whereby the boys were to engage in musical studies in the morning and evening and attend to their general education during the afternoon, is a little redolent of choir schools. In a sense Defoe's proposals foreshadowed the choir school of Sir Frederick Gore Ouseley of St. Michael's College, Tenbury in Worcestershire in the nineteenth century since Ouseley's school was formed on a blue-print rather than evolving like other choir schools.[21] Defoe might be considered by some to be educationally naive when he recommended the curtailment of school holidays. Defoe suggested holidays "cannot be too few, considering what a hindrance they are to juvenile studies. It is a vulgar error," he wrote, "that has too long prevail'd all over *England*, to the great detriment of learning, and many boys have been made blockheads, in complaisance to Kings and Saints, dead for many ages past." Defoe was himself such an indefatigable worker that the Catholic recognition of saints' days, a relic of pre-reformation days, offended his Protestant ethic.

It was his earlier work, *An Essay upon Projects* (1697), which had won for Defoe a reputation for inventive genius. He is more concerned in the *Essay* with projects which have a financial aspect. Hence his thoughts dwell on county banks, friendly societies, a pension office and a bankruptcy commission. Fiscal though *An Essay upon Projects* may predominantly be, it nevertheless contains projects which are the concern of educationists. Chief among these is his proposal for an academy for women, to which reference has already been made in Chapter 3. His basic premise behind this proposal was Platonic and Vivesque:[22] that the genetic endowment of women was such that they stood as equals to men in their potential to benefit from education and that to leave them uneducated was a waste. Defoe went even further—he entertained thoughts of the capacities of women being greater and their senses quicker than those of men.

In his proposals for the education of women, Defoe did not have in mind girls' schools but educational seminaries for women, one for each county and ten in the City of London. He gave lengthy consideration to the proprieties of his proposals which went beyond those of a contemporary work, *Advice to the Ladies*, suggesting that the educational provision should be different from that given in a nunnery. Defoe proposed that women should study together in a house provided for the purpose, within a walled garden to minimise male interference. He affirmed that such an academy would be run like a public school and that women who so wished to be educated would enrol for a whole year for which fees would be received and not refunded irrespective of their early withdrawal through possible liaisons. Here Defoe was applying strict business principles to an educational proposition.

The curriculum suggested by Defoe went beyond the usual accomplishments of Music and Dancing studied by ladies. True to his belief in their genetic endowments, Defoe advocated their study of foreign languages, especially French and Italian. History, too, he regarded as suitable for study by women. His remarks on the curriculum were, however, sparing so that his only other advice was that no subject should be denied those women who had the genius for it. Science and Mathematics presumably would not be denied to women in Defoe's proposed academy.

Defoe proposed other educational projects which aimed at providing (i) an academy to safeguard the development of the English language similar in function to that of L'Académie Française; and (ii) academies for military studies which would recognize the then recent fundamental changes in warfare. Defoe, the author of *Memoirs of a Cavalier* (1720), had in fact, been intensely interested in military matters and devoted more space to his military academies than to the academies for women. As a young man he had fought at Sedgemoor for the Duke of Monmouth and as confidant to William III he had shared military discussions with the martial monarch, including a plan, as already noted, for the take-over of Spanish colonies in the West Indies at the beginning of the War of the Spanish Succession. This interest in military studies was evidenced also in his *Review* where he bemoaned the lack of engineering studies at the universities, which put the English at a disadvantage in siege warfare.[23]

The Education of the Deaf and Dumb

The evident interest in the education of the deaf and dumb formed part of that widening of Defoe's mental horizons which occurred after the apparent submersion of his political interests with the institution of the Hanoverian succession in 1714. This later period was marked by his innovative writing of novels, his interest in social aspects of life including education, and his interest in magic and the occult and in possible new projects designed to enhance the quality of life by the suppression of crime and other nuisances.

Defoe first showed a public interest in the dumb when he wrote *The Dumb Philosopher* (1719) which was concerned with Dickory Cronke, a Cornishman who was dumb for most of his life but regained his speech just before his death. The work has some significance for this present study as it shows the links between Defoe's interest in the dumb and his interest in the occult, since Dickory Cronke was given to prophesy before he died. There is, therefore, a link between this human affliction and the occult which recurs in Defoe's later work *The Supernatural Philosopher* (1728), the full title of which clearly indicates the links between the deaf and dumb, their education and the occult or world of inexplicable phenomena.

There is some doubt about the authorship of the work entitled *The History of the Life and Adventures of Mr. Duncan Campbell* (1720) which contains an exegesis of a method for teaching the deaf and dumb. It has been attributed to William Bond by some scholars since *The Supernatural Philosopher*, which incorporates the *History of the Life and Adventures of Mr. Duncan Campbell*, has also been attributed to William Bond. This mystery and confusion could be occasioned by no more than Defoe's penchant for anonymity in his later years. The evidence for his authorship of Mr. Duncan Campbell's history is fairly strong if its proximity in time to *The Dumb Philosopher* is taken into account and also Defoe's acquaintance with the famous teacher of the deaf and dumb, Mr. Henry Baker, from 1724 onwards, who in 1729 became his son-in-law by marrying Defoe's daughter, Sophie. Despite the lingering doubts about Defoe's authorship of the *History of Mr. Duncan Campbell* and despite the demonstrated association of the deaf and dumb with inexplicable phenomena, this interest places Defoe well among those who have shown a keen interest in the learning process. Although not an adviser in this field since he confesses not to understand the mechanisms by which the deaf and dumb learn, he is an intermediary for the giving of advice, when in both the *History of Mr. Duncan Campbell* and *The Supernatural Philosopher* he publicizes methods of Dr. Wallis for teaching the deaf and dumb. Defoe's study of the learning process in the deaf and dumb led him to the educational insight that, as with children who are not handicapped, natural ability is required for substantial progress to be made. The fact that the deaf and dumb were often able to master alternative modes of communication demonstrated their capabilities. Defoe appreciated that handicaps such as this serve to enhance rather than depress individual achievement.

Defoe's very evident interest in the education of the deaf and dumb became apparent once more in Defoe's *Mere Nature Delineated* (1726) where he considered Peter the Wild Boy who was recently found in a 'natural' condition in German woods. Defoe raised the similar problems faced by his friend and future son-in-law Mr. Henry Baker when applying education to mere nature with those deaf and dumb children submitted to his care. In *The Compleat English Gentleman* Defoe briefly raised the difficulties encountered by the deaf at least in the process of learning.[24]

Reference has already been made in Chapter 3 to Defoe's criticism of the education of dissenting ministers in the academies of the late seventeenth and early eighteenth centuries. It was noted that though Defoe was a critic of the academies he was also very much their friend. As an alumnus of Dr. Morton's academy, he was a publicist for dissenting academies and throughout his literary career praised their efforts and defended their rights. This loyalty to the dissenters despite their misapprehensions of him, is all the more enhanced by comparing his consistent adherence to their principles with the defection, to the Church of England, of Samuel Wesley the elder (1662-1735), a fellow pupil of Defoe at Dr. Morton's Academy, who joined Exeter College, Oxford, as a student in 1683. Defoe's consistency with Dissent, if sometimes a little obscured by his enforced duplicity, weakens the arguments of those critics who see in him a man of expedience only. From the Dissenters' cause, despite seeming evidence to the contrary, particularly with *The Shortest Way with the Dissenters*, Defoe never wavered. He was their constant watchdog.

In 1704 Defoe joined in a controversy concerning dissenting academies between Samuel Palmer (d. 1724), then a Presbyterian minister, and Samuel Wesley, the elder. Wesley had written a scathing attack on non-conformist academies in 1693, entitled *A Letter from a country divine to his friend in London concerning the education of dissenters in their private academies, in several parts of this nation*, published in 1703. Samuel Palmer had leapt to the defence of the academies in his pamphlet *A defence of the dissenters' education in their private academies in answer to Mr. W——y's disingenuous reflections upon 'em* published in the same year. This pamphlet warfare became more acerbic when Wesley replied to Palmer with his *A defence of a letter concerning the education of dissenters in their private academies; with a more full and satisfactory account of the same, and of their morals and behaviour towards the Church of England: being an answer to the defence of dissenters' education* (1704). It was at this point that Defoe jumped into the fray with a blistering attack on Wesley's logic in which the dissenting academies had been attacked and found wanting on the grounds of some of their less-than-perfect pupils being less than perfect. He rebutted Wesley's charges of anti-monarchial sentiment by reminding him of his own school days at Dr. Morton's Academy. He declared that dissenting academies were open to inspection by anyone and that the only reason for their existence was the exclusion of dissenters from the universities. He wrote:

Open a Door to us in your Universities, and let our youth be fairly admitted to Study there, without imposing Oaths and Obligations upon them, and it shall no more be said that we erect Schools in opposition to you.[25]

He went on:

But while you shut our Children out of your Schools, never Quarrel at our Teaching them at Schools of our own, or sending 'em into Foreign Countries to be Taught, since wherever they are Taught they generally get a share of Learning, at least equal to yourselves.[26]

This objective of Dissenters obtaining entry to the universities was in evidence, too, in an article in his *Review* on 27th December 1705, when he wrote "what tho' the Sacramental Test be not taken off, nor our children allow'd to study in the public universities?" A year later Defoe was chiding those who, while claiming to uphold toleration to Dissenters, sought to close Dissenters' schools.[27] Defoe ridiculed the asininity of this ambivalent policy. The threat was to become a reality in 1714, and Defoe, in *The Weakest go to the Wall* (1714), was to denounce the reality of the Schism Act in much the same terms as the assumed threat in 1706. Meanwhile Samuel Palmer had taken up cudgels again with Samuel Wesley in 1705 with his *A vindication of the learning, loyalty, morals and most Christian behaviour of the dissenters towards the Church of England, in answer to Mr. Wesley's defence of his letter concerning the dissenters' education in their private academies, and to Mr. Sacheverell's injurious reflections upon them.* Wesley replied to this in his *A reply to Mr. Palmer's vindication of the learning, loyalty, morals and most Christian behaviour of the dissenters towards the Church of England* in 1707. It would seem that not only did Wesley get the last word in this religious conflict but also won the day insofar as Palmer defected to the Church of England and became vicar of All Saints' and St. Peter's, Maldon from 1710 to his death in 1724. Defoe was not to be so easily vanquished.

In *The Present State of the Parties in Great Britain* (1712), Defoe alluded to the Palmer-Wesley controversy of previous years and to Palmer's subsequent defection,[28] before going on to offer advice on improving the education of dissenting ministers, the defects of which were examined in Chapter 3. Using Dr. Morton's Academy at Newington Green as a model, Defoe advised on English as being the medium of teaching. His other suggestions were designed to meet the weaknesses he had already analysed. He strongly advised on an adequate time being allowed for the education of future dissenting ministers; for the limiting of numbers of recruits to the ministry so that quality rather than quantity became the guiding principle; and for inspectors to be appointed to inspect the standards within the academies and the suitability of the candidates.[29] This last suggestion was indeed a radical one since it presupposed some kind of co-ordination between dissenting academies. A further suggestion by Defoe ought possibly to be of interest to educationists in the twentieth century who wrestle with the problems of equality of opportunity and those of differentiation. Defoe, in his advice to his fellow Dissenters, suggested the recruitment of boys from more wealthy families since in his view they were more likely to be successful Dissenting ministers.[30] The complementary point was made again by Defoe in *Wise as Serpents* (1712) where he stated that some Dissenting ministers "having been by the Charity of the Dissenters supported, have had an Education as sparing and narrow as the Charity of the Times seems to portend."[31]

The Schism Act of 1714 which forbade Dissenters from keeping school and which was nominally in force until its repeal in 1719, was instrumental in bringing out the best of Defoe's guardian instinct. In an article in *Review of the State of the British Nation*,[32] Defoe had compared the plight of the Huguenots in France with that of the Dissenters in England and had wondered whether or not the Dissenters, like the Huguenots, would be deprived of their schools. He had expressed similar sentiments in *The Weakest go to the Wall* (1714). The Schism Act of 1714 made this a reality. Defoe had written twice to the Earl of Oxford before the passing of the Schism Bill endeavouring to strengthen his opposition against Bolingbroke's hostile measure, but Oxford was by then in no position to affect the situation. Consequently in no less than four pamphlets that year Defoe leapt to the defence of dissenting academies and attacked the Schism Act tooth and nail. In *The Remedy worse than the Disease* (1714), Defoe attacked the monopoly in education which robbed dissenting parents of the right to educate their children how they wished, as well as of the legal control of knowledge. In a more positive vein he strongly supported the concept of variety in education and suggested that varied schools were a safeguard of Liberty, in much the same way as independent schools today argue the value of their independence, to the nation generally. *En passant*, Defoe warned that the implementation of the Schism Act would lead to a diminution of the charity schools since some of them were dissenting charity schools.

Defoe's *Brief survey of the legal liberties of the Dissenters* (1714) concentrated on the effects of the Schism Act and the ambivalence of policy which continued to allow toleration but closed schools whereby that toleration could be extended. The Act would have the effect of drastically diminishing dissenters' charity since many would now have to spend money on the education of their children abroad; it would have the effect of propagating ignorance; and have adverse effects on the living standards of teachers many of whom would be deprived of their livelihood.[33] It was in the light of these new religious handicaps that Defoe appealed to Richard Steele as a person of some influence, in *A Letter to Mr. Steele* (1714).

One bright star in a dull firmament, as seen through the eyes of Defoe, was his *Memoirs of the Life and Eminent Conduct of that Learned and Reverend Divine Daniel Williams D.D.* (1718), in which he acknowledged the great advantage which would accrue to future recruits to the dissenting ministry, arising from the bequeathal of Dr. Williams' Library. Dr. Williams was a wealthy benefactor and left a large library which still bears his name.[34] In this way Defoe complemented Miss M. G. Jones, insofar as, in *The Charity School Movement*, she stressed Dr. Williams' contribution to that movement: while Defoe emphasized Dr. Williams' contribution to the cause of dissenting academies. Neither alluded to the other's main concern.

Finally, in his support of dissenting education Defoe never forgot the value of his own education at Newington Green. When considering the absence of scholarship among the English gentry he could turn to no better model than Dr. Morton in search of a remedy. Who else could fit Defoe's scholastic allusion in *The Compleat English Gentleman* when he referred to a tutor of his former acquaintance? He wrote:

> I once was acquainted with a tutor of unquestion'd reputacion for learning and who was himself a critick in the learned languages and even in all the oriental tongues, as the Syriac, Chaldee, Arabic, Hebrew; and none could object that he did it for want of skill, but being sencible of the great defficiency I have been speaking of, and how our gentlemen were dropt, as it were, out of the conversation of the learned world, he set up what he call'd an English Accademy.[35]

Charity Schools

As is made clear in *The Great Law of Subordination Considered* (1714), Defoe had a typical middle rank view of the poor recognizing their station in life. Such a view was as philanthropic in character as it was selfish, since it was based on a belief in happiness arising in a situation where an individual is fulfilling an accepted function or station. The Aristotelian idea of $\varepsilon\upsilon\delta\alpha\iota\mu o\nu\iota\alpha$ arising from $\varepsilon\nu\tau\varepsilon\lambda\varepsilon X\iota\alpha$ was a generally, if unconsciously, accepted premise. For this reason Defoe had approved of charity schools and was supportive of their objectives, especially when their educational endeavour was being threatened by government taxation. In his *Review of the State of the British Nation* of 29th April 1712, Defoe showed concern for the work of the S.P.C.K. which was being threatened by rises in paper tax. He warned his readers of the deleterious effects such a tax would have upon the task of educating the poor.

Such advocacy of the cause of charity schools, however, was mild in the light of the intense controversy Defoe found himself engaged in seven years later when, in keeping with his supposed Tory sympathies, he attacked those who were endeavouring to prevent the preaching of Charity School sermons on behalf of St. Anne Charity School, Aldersgate. The affair was a political storm in a religious tea-cup insofar as the opponents of the charity school sermons believed that collections were being made for Jacobite purposes. In *Charity Still a Christian Virtue* (1719) Defoe harangued those who tried to prevent a sermon being preached at Chislehurst in Kent, recording for posterity a blow-by-blow history of such an explosive incident. Defoe insisted on the legality of charity schools and the objectives of charity school sermons, emphasizing the benefits to be derived from such sermons. He was in one sense acting out of character, since as a Dissenter he would not normally be interested in the fate of Anglican charity schools. Perhaps the solution to this discrepancy lies in the recognition that Defoe was as much interested in the social law of subordination as he was in establishing heterodox religious principles of non-conformity. He could be said to have plumped for social orthodoxy at the expense of religious heterodoxy in his defence of Charity Schools in *Applebee's Journal*, twice during one week in 1723.[36]

Summary

In addition to being a critic of education, Defoe was also a strong advocate, in more than one sense, of education. Over a long period of time from 1697 to his death in 1731, he felt disposed to throw out ideas on education which have since found general acceptance. Sandhurst, London University and the Royal Academy of Music are educational institutions which were foreshadowed by Defoe, the great projector. He took an active interest, too, in that very specialist area of education—the teaching of the deaf and dumb. Moreover, when educational institutions like charity schools and dissenting academies were under criticism they found a no more redoubtable advocate to argue their case than Daniel Defoe. He was their forthright champion. As far as the dissenting academies and charity schools were concerned, his role was similar to that of a legal advocate, but he was also an advocate of eductional principles. It is to the nature of those educational principles that our attention will now be turned.

CHAPTER 5

Defoe's Educational Tenets

The examination of Defoe's educational ideas has so far been related to Defoe's reactions to existing educational institutions or situations. His criticism or advocacy of education examined in Chapters 3 and 4 respectively have related largely to the educational context in which he found himself. It will be readily recognized, however, that educational thinkers entertain ideas which transcend the immediate context and perhaps can be examined in isolation. A distinction can therefore be made between 'pragmatic' and 'transcendental' educational ideas. Defoe's ideas for example on 'natural ability' or 'genius' do not relate only to the eighteenth century but can be considered also in the twentieth-century context, however naive those ideas may seem. On the other hand, his views on the desirability or otherwise of charity schools for the enforcement of his great law of subordination are not likely to have more than historical interest in times of mass secular education. It could be debated, even in this instance, whether or not principles *per se* are involved. Be that as it may, Chapters 3 and 4 have been concerned with Defoe's reactions to educational situations: this chapter is concerned with educational principles or tenets which Defoe held.

Before an examination of these principles it is as well to recognize difficulties which were foreshadowed in Chapter 1. The line between reactions to situations and principles is not very clear; the one merges into the other, but the context for each (if indeed there is a context for the latter) is even less clear. Take for example the education of women in the paradigm adopted in this monograph. Defoe's criticism of the lack of women's education and his advocacy of it form complementary parts of a contextual situation, but it is possible to express this also as an educational principle arising from the context. In other words the general Defoean principle is abstracted from the particular Defoean situation: its generation is dependent upon the context but its enunciation requires to be free of all contextual trammels. The problem lies in discerning at what point a principle or tenet has thus been freed to be a principle *per se* and in deciding whether or not there is benefit in a juxtaposition of the context with the principle to enhance the latter. In the examination of Defoe's educational principles some will be contextually supported: some will not.

A good sub-title for this sub-section of the chapter might be 'some eight-eenth-century insights into the modern nature versus nurture controversy.' Where would Defoe stand in such a controversy? Some indication has al-ready been given at the beginning of Chapter 3. At least five of his major works made his position quite clear and perhaps give guidance to those who seem intent on polarizing their position or, even more unwisely, who try to quantify the respective contributions of nature and nurture. Defoe believed in the value of 'genetic' nature but he also was a strong advocate of educa-tional nurture.

Early in his literary career, in *An Essay upon Projects* (1697), his strenu-ous advocacy of the education of women was based first of all on a belief in their very adequate (even superior) natural endowment and secondly on the need for enhancing this through education. He stated:

> The Soul is plac'd in the Body like a rough Diamond and must be pol-ish'd, or the lustre of it will never appear: and 'tis manifest that as the Rational Soul distinguishes us from Brutes, so Education carries on the distinction, and makes some less brutish than others: This is too evident to need any demonstration.[1]

Defoe's recognition of the need for nurture to enhance nature is again strongly in evidence when he concerns himself with proposals for a military academy. Taking for granted presumably an aggressive instinct in man, the *raison d'être* for such an institution was that

> Soldiers, Horsemen, Engineers, Gunners and the like, must be bred and taught; men are not born with Muskets on their Shoulders, nor Fortifica-tions in their Heads.[2]

In *The Present State of the Parties in Great Britain* (1712) Defoe seems to concentrate more on natural endowment or lack of endowment, concern-ing himself with the folly of trying to educate beyond the limits of that en-dowment. Defoe warned against the wasted effort involved in teaching those who have insufficient natural ability to benefit from it. Thus he echoed the educational aphorism of Sir Henry Wotton, "Every Nature is not a fit stock to graft a scholar on."[3] Such a view is the antithesis of the philosophy of the first *Newsom Report* (1963) when, the then Minister of Education, Sir Ed-ward (now Lord) Boyle, wrote in the introductory preface about opportuni-ties for "*acquiring* intelligence" (my italics). Boyle's view was more in tune with that of Helvétius than of Defoe. Rather than entertaining a certain sensitivity about academic limitations which leads to such euphemisms as 'special education' or 'education of the less able,' Defoe is blunt in his writing and with pachydermatous indifference refers to 'blockheads' and 'fools.' Such a view if adopted as a national policy would possibly bring about economies in educational expenditure since demands on funds for education would be substantially less.

The work in which Defoe engaged in extensive speculation of Nature or natural abilities was in his *Mere Nature Delineated*, published in 1726, following the discovery of Peter the Wild Boy who had, it was alleged, been reared by wolves near Hamelin, in Hanover. The discovery of this eighteenth-century edition of either Romulus or Remus was the subject of much speculation among those writers and thinkers who were concerned with Nature and its relation to the artificiality of civilization. As Defoe observed,

> He seems to be the very Creature which the learned World have, for many Years past, pretended to wish for, viz one that being kept entirely from human Society, so as never to have heard anyone speak, must therefore either not speak at all, or, if he did form any Speech to himself, then they should know what Language Nature would first form for Mankind.[4]

Defoe was anxious in *Mere Nature Delineated* to make his readers aware of the speculative issues arising from this unique opportunity; but although he made one astute observation about lack of discrimination in the untutored mind he was nevertheless out of his depth. He showed a healthy curiosity about questions of conceptual psychology arising from the non-possession of language, but while recognizing that words are the medium of thought he was puzzled about the thinking of those who have no words and could not give his readers any plausible solution. Defoe's conception of the state of Peter the Wild Boy's mind was quaint indeed by twentieth-century levels of psychological knowledge. He looked upon him in his natural state as a machine that had not been exercised or educated. This conception of Peter's natural state led Defoe to speculate on both the value of early education and pedagogic instruction. (His views on these will be considered in succeeding sub-sections.) He concluded that "an untaught Man, a Creature in human Shape, but intirely neglected and uninstructed is ten thousand times more miserable than a Brute."[5] In this way Defoe was a critic of mere nature and an advocate of education.

The two fragmentary treatises on education which were left unpublished by Defoe confirmed his views on Nature and Education, already examined in earlier works. In his concern for the widespread ignorance of the English gentry, Defoe suggested in *The Compleat English Gentleman* that too often sons of gentry were left in a state of mere nature. In one dialogue between two sons, one declared that "The gifts of nature are not learnt at school."

To which the other replied: "They are improv'd at school: those rough diamonds are polished by the schools and by the help of books and instruccion."[6]

If in *An Essay upon Projects* Defoe were concerned with female self-realization and if in *The Present State of the Parties in Great Britain*, with limited natural abilities, in *The Compleat English Gentleman* he was concerned with the corollary of those two—individual differentiation. He wrote:

> I am content to allow that, as some men are born dull . . . so on the other hand, some are born bright, have a sprightly wit, a great genius, a capacious soul, deep reach and clear thoughts even from their birth.[7]

Defoe did admit, however, that sometimes this hereditary gift is inexplicable in view of the family history, even going back generations. He continued:

> Thus the bright genius, the naturall beauty of the mind, the parts, the witt, the capascities given by Nature to one youth, cause him to be polish'd and cultivated with more ease, and he is finish'd with fewer hands in less time and with much less difficulty than another crooked, knotty, stubborn disposition, which being naturally dul and awkward requires much more hewing and shapeing and dressing.[8]

Moll Flanders, for example, was naturally bright as she discovered when she benefited indirectly from the education given to the daughters of the house in which Moll was a servant. As Moll noted, "in some things I had the advantage of my ladies, though they were my superiors, viz., that mine were all gifts of nature, and which all their fortunes could not furnish."[9] Defoe made a strong plea for the education at an early stage of those who were discovered to be "bright." Teaching was necessary if such bright children were to be fully developed for as Defoe averred "nature is the best fund, yet the dictates of nature are not the best guides."[10]

Acknowledging this differentiation of ability Defoe in *Of Royall Educacion* suggested that so often high ability is to be found in the offspring of the royal and noble parentage, which led him to the conclusion that education was all the more needed by them. He wrote:

> by how much the greater the nativ lustre, the reall intrinsick beauty and excellence there may be suggested in the souls of men nobly born and of men destin'd for glory, than is found in others of inferior rank: by so much the greater should the skill and care be which ought to be used in the educacion of such persons . . .[11]

Such a view is diametrically opposed to modern practice which by comparison neglects relatively the education of the gifted in the interests of the many.

A strong advocacy of education *per se* could be Rousseauvian in character, or traditional. If largely Rousseauvian its emphasis is on learning through the senses and recognizing education as deriving from the Latin *'educere,'* 'to lead out.' If largely traditional, the emphasis is likely to be on an early start to formal education, with instruction forming an important part and a recognition of the Latin *'educare,'* 'to mould.' If these are the basic characteristics of two approaches to education, then Defoe must be regarded as a traditionalist. In *The Compleat English Gentleman* he wrote:

> all the mischiefs of a young gentleman's education are occasion'd by a neglect of the most early instruccions: The principles of vertue, religion and subjeccion to government are to be planted in the minds of children from the very first moments that they can be made capable of recieving them, that they may be sure to have the first possession of their minds . . .[12]

This Piagetian concept of readiness for early education is to be found in Defoe's earlier work, *The Family Instructor* (1715), in which he suggested that five or six was a suitable age for the formal education of a child when it is "thinking and enquiring."[13] That heavily moralistic and didactic volume was widely received by Defoe's contemporaries, running in fact into ten editions in sixteen years. According to some commentators a copy of it could be found in every humble cottage in the land and Benjamin Franklin attested to its popularity.[14] It has been claimed, too, that its popularity extended to the royal household of George I.[15] This is unlikely, since George II, the son of George I, was born in 1683 and was therefore thirty-one or thirty-two at the time of *The Family Instructor*'s publication.[16] It is possible, however, that Frederick Louis (1707-1751) Prince of Wales and grandson of George I benefited from the presence of *The Family Instructor* in the royal household. Whatever is the case, there is little doubt that *The Family Instructor* was a widely received didactic work which advocated an early education.

This view of the need for early education was consistent with Defoe's views expressed eleven years later in his *Mere Nature Delineated* where he wrote in Lockean fashion that:

> If this be the Case, it dictates the Necessity of early Education of Children, in whom, not the Soul only but the organick Powers are, as a Lump of soft Wax, which is always ready to receive any Impression; but if harden'd, grow callous, and stubborn, and like what we call Sealing-Wax, obstinately refuse the Impression of the Seal, unless melted and reduced by the Force of Fire; that is to say, Unless moulded and temper'd to Instruction, Length of Time and abundance of Difficulty.[17]

But although Defoe adopts the Lockean motif of a *tabula rasa* or wax tablet he differs from Locke in his attitude to young children's education. Locke would advise that reason be applied in the handling of children but Defoe is convinced of the need to stamp out original sin which children display when naughty and Locke's waxen analogy in Defoe's hands becomes a rationale for traditional strict discipline.

Reference has already been made to Defoe's repetitive criticism of the lack of education among the English gentry. Much of the blame for this lacuna in education is put firmly at the door of female responsibility since mothers and nurses too often neglect the early education of the young. He wrote,

> those directresses in his most early yeares who for want of erudition have exposed him to ignorance and weakness of understanding and left his head unfurnish'd and his mind unfinish'd. . . .[18]

The Relations between Parents and Children

Defoe's attitude towards the question of the relationship between parents and children was modified over a period of time. This modification may have arisen from Defoe's own experiences in life but there undoubtedly was a shift of emphasis. From *The Family Instructor* (1715), where he writes not only about parental duty to children,[19] but also about filial affection to parents, he moves in *A Protestant Monastery* (1726) and *Chickens Feed Capons* (1731), towards a position of hostility towards those sons and daughters who are inconsiderate to their parents. It is as if Defoe's philosophy about parental and filial relations had become soured through bitter experience.

In the second volume of *The Family Instructor* (1718) he wrote about affection "that endearing part which alone unites the souls of parents and children." Defoe used epithets like 'dear' and 'tender' parent and 'loving,' 'dutiful' and 'affectionate' child to describe this familial social contract. But already, in an earlier work, in *Conduct of Christians made the Sport of Infidels* (1717), Defoe felt constrained to attack the lack of respect for parents by some children. Such behaviour he felt to be unnatural. In observing the customs of Islam he noted:

> The just Authority as well as Reverence of Parents, being kept sacred by the Instinct of Affections proceeding from Nature's Oeconomy in Man's Soul, are likewise preserv'd secure and uninvaded by the *Mussulman's* Law.[20]

According to Defoe it would seem Islam was more strict than Christianity in this respect since "the rebelling Son who insults his Parents, receives his due

Reward at the Hand of the Executioner."[21] Such a Draconi
advocated by Defoe but in his later works, viz., *The Prote*
and *Chickens Feed Capons,* Defoe seems to be truly disapp
In *The Protestant Monastery* he pointed to the cruelty of s
"triumph in the Strength of their Youth, and snuff their
Age: Who laugh at the Groanings of the hoary Head, and
of Compassion for the Bowels that gave them Nourishment."
parents and adults for dereliction of duty when they left
cruel tendencies in the young. He encouraged everyone to
when they were "taunting and flouncing at their Parents, '
lations" and mocking others either for their old age or their
Chickens Feed Capons, Defoe endeavoured to gain respect
the old by reminding youth of the Biblical injunction 'Ho
and thy Mother' and with the Christian aphorism, 'do as
done by' since at some time the youth of today would be tt
morrow and grandparents thereafter. Clearly Defoe's views
soured over the years, after beginning with tender hopes fo

The Family and Education

In times of modern state-provided education, it is custo
the family to a low position as an educational institution. I
fare state there is a tendency for the family's position in ed
the very early years, to be eroded by the provision of da
kindergartens. Gradually Plato's *Laws* is becoming a reality
vided crèches. In the eighteenth century, on the other ha
education and with the churches providing education for a
it was customary for the lower orders not to expect educatic
of the wealthy to be educated at home, that is if it were re
sary: so often, as Defoe bemoaned, it was not.

In outlining his ideal of a *Compleat English Gentlen*
gested that if a gentleman had children then "his *princi*
education" (my italics).[24] Contrary to contemporary practic
the eldest son of such a family to receive no education but t
affairs of the estate, Defoe suggested that it was the duty of
man to ensure the instruction not only of his younger son
eldest son.

It is with the two volumes of *The Family Instructor* (171
The New Family Instructor (1727) that Defoe establishes
of the family's role in the educational process. It has been

successful Defoe's *Family Instructor* was. It would seem to have been a
essful competitor with that other eighteenth-century 'best-seller,' *The
ıle Duty of Man* which according to the title page (19th edition 1763)
"*Necessary for all families*, and authorized by the King's most excellent
esty" (not my italics). Defoe asserted in his first volume of the *Family
ructor* that is was natural for parents to be responsible for the education
heir children and that a neglect of this duty was likely to store up trou-
for the future when such children became aware of how they had been
ected.[26] Defoe was more condemnatory of those parents who were suffi-
tly knowledgeable to educate their own children but neglected to do so.
first two volumes of the *Family Instructor* assume education taking place
ıin the family through the efforts either of the mother or of a
rness. The *New Family Instructor*, on the other hand, assumes the fa-
's responsibility during the later development of the children; as the pref-
states "The Instructor here is the Master of a Family, whose Business
Duty is to inform and confirm his Children in right Principles."[27] It
unfortunate, Defoe observed, that so many families failed to be educated
tly because parents shunned instruction and partly because children were
etimes insufficiently curious to want to know. This could not be said of
e of Defoe's fictional characters, especially Colonel Jack. Defoe, at least,
a strong advocate of education, and in the three volumes under consid-
ion, education within the family. It has been customary for commenta-
on Defoe to account for Defoe's entry in 1715 into didactic and moralis-
literature (which antedates both *Emile* and *How Gertrude Teaches her
ldren*) as an attempt to make up for a worldly life. The work coincided
ı an illness that made Defoe, whose constitution had always been very
ust, think of his entry into the next world. *The Family Instructor* has
n explained, therefore, in terms of expiation. It is possible, however, to
ount for *The Family Instructor* in a different way since it purported to be
nanual of family instruction at a time when Dissenters were being de-
ved of the freedom of running their own schools. The *Schism Act* which
nominally in force from 1714 to 1719 could therefore account not only
volume I (1715) but also volume II (1718), while the gap between the
earance of the second volume and the publication of the *New Family
tructor* can be accounted for in terms of decreasing sectarian need after
9 and possible increasing financial worries in his later years. This last
nt is very much conjecture since the last years of Defoe are wrapped
ıewhat in obscurity. He certainly had attained new wealth from his pop-
r writings, but although his wealth increased so did his creditors who

66

forced him finally to go into hiding to avoid a repetition of his earlier Newgate experience.

Ironically enough, it was in terms of 'creditors' that Defoe in *Serious Reflections of Robinson Crusoe* (1720) saw a man's wife and children in relation to himself. He wrote:

> A Wife and Children are Creditors to the Father of the Family; and he cannot be an honest Man that does not discharge his Debt to them. . . .[28]

The *first* debt which a man owed to his children was their education. Defoe expounded at some length on this principal debt. He wrote:

> As first, EDUCATION: By this I mean, not only putting Children to School, which some Parents think, is all they have to do with or for their Children; and indeed with some, is all that they know how to do, or are fit to do: I say, I do not mean this only, but several other additional Cares, as (1) Directing what School, what parts of learning, is proper for them, what Improvements they are to be taught (2) studying the Genius and Capacities of their Children, in what they teach them: Some Children will voluntarily learn one Thing, and can never be forc'd to learn another; and for Want of which observing the Genius of Children, we have so many learned Blockheads in the World, who are mere Scholars, Pedants and no more (3) But the main Part of this Debt, which Relative Honesty calls upon us to pay to our Children, is the Debt of Instruction, the Debt of Government, the Debt of Example: he that neglects to pay any of these to his Family is a *relative knave*. (Defoe's italics)[29]

Defoe recognized a second debt which parents owe to their children in addition to education. This second debt is what Defoe called 'induction' recognizing that "the debt from a parent is far from ending when the children come from school." Unlike much of the rest of the animal kingdom, where the young are heaved from the nest as soon as they are relatively mobile, man is responsible for ensuring a successful induction into the children's future world. This process of induction involves for the parent a close examination of the capacities of the child so that its talents are put to best use. No doubt Defoe was in deadly earnest in making his point, but it cannot go unnoticed that certain aspects of this advocacy are subconsciously autobiographical since Defoe himself was to have followed a different career if his father had had his way. The divergence of aim between Daniel and James Foe about Defoe's future career has led some commentators to see *Robinson Crusoe* as an autobiography of Defoe in emblematic form since among other similarities, there is a similar divergence of aim, in the novel, between father and son when Robinson Crusoe insists on going to sea. Such speculations are of only marginal interest for this monograph. The important point was that

Defoe saw the family's responsibility to children being both *education* and *induction*.

Education of Women

Defoe's advocacy of the education of women has been a continuing theme. He was both critical of their educational neglect and a forceful adviser in remedying this neglect in *An Essay upon Projects*. In view of the attention given to the education of women in Chapters 3 and 4, it merely remains to record the elevation of this aspect of education as an educational principle in a chapter concerned with Defoe's educational tenets or principles. Certainly Defoe would see the education of women as not only having intrinsic worth but also as having instrumental value since the education of the young is likely to be more beneficial at the hands of an educated, rather than an ignorant, mother. In this sense, the effects of girls' education are farther reaching than those of boys. Defoe concluded his essay on the education of women[30] with the hope for "those happy days, if ever they shall be, when men shall be wise enough to mend" the neglect of women's education, so convinced was he of this educational necessity.

Christian Education

English and American historians have been wont to refer to the eighteenth century as the period of the Enlightenment. Similarly French historians in deference to the *philosophes* have referred to this period as 'l'éclaircissement.' In Germany, late in the century, Kant asked the question '*Was ist Aufklärung?*' and came to the conclusion, paradoxically, that although the eighteenth century was an age of Enlightenment it was not an enlightened age. No doubt his negative outlook was determined largely by the still savage and cruel age which caused the polite French and German salons, and the intellectual gathering of *philosophes* to be rather like beacons of light in a dark night. In the view of some of the *philosophes*, religion constituted part of that darkness since religious dogma was partly the object of their enlightened criticism. In their view Reason dispelled the darkness of unreasoning Faith. Such a view, however, which saw a gulf between Reason and Faith, was a minority view. The eighteenth century despite its being an age of enlightenment was an age of religion in which Reason was also the way to religion and God. *The Whole Duty of Man* exemplified this when, discussing immortality, it stated "the arguments from reason are taken from the nature of the soul itself."[31] As this popular religious work affirmed at a later stage, "when we are satisfied that a doctrine is revealed by God, though it is above

68

the reach of our understanding; yet we have the strongest and most cogent reason in the world to believe it: because God is infinitely wise and all-knowing, and therefore cannot be deceived."[32] In this context, Defoe was a man of his eighteenth-century world, a man of mundane reason and a religious man. Sometimes eighteenth-century England has been regarded as not being very religious. It is true that 'enthusiasm,' at least during the early part of it, was discouraged as being an undesirable quality, but in Georgian England religion did flourish, even if a religious movement like Methodism could not be accommodated till the latter part of the century.

During the early years, however, there was considerable activity in the churches, engaged in Christian charity. The Society for Promoting Christian Knowledge was closely engaged for thirty years in serving as an advice bureau for the setting up of charity schools in various parts of the country and facilitating opportunities of charitable work among England's middling ranks of society. Such philanthropy became ripe for satire at the pen of Bernard Mandeville in *The Fable of the Bees*. Defoe, too, had attacked, in *Giving Alms no Charity* (1704), the policy of Sir Humphrey Mackworth (1657-1727), a capitalist M.P., for organizing charity and the relief of the poor which would in the end have the effect of putting out of work some of those already employed. Defoe's quarrel with Mackworth arose not from a difference of religious viewpoint, but from an economic one. Mackworth was either a whited sepulchre or one whose mundane capitalist interests were stronger than his altruistic Christian principles since he was found guilty, by the House of Commons in 1710, of peculation. Be that as it may, Defoe, Mackworth's adversary in charity, was as religious in nature as he was experienced in commerce and trade.

This religious aspect of Defoe is to be found in many of his writings and obtrudes even into his novels where his heroes and heroines have fits of piety or contrite remorse, according to the overall quality of their lives. *Moll Flanders* concludes, for instance, with the "resolve to spend the remainder of [her] years in sincere penitence," while Robinson Crusoe was made to reflect on his desert island upon the righteousness and omnipotence of God, to whom he offered total obedience.[33] This all-pervading religious sentiment was present in eighteenth-century educational enterprises. Both in the dissenting academies and the charity schools, religion was an integral part of education. Education was, in fact, Christian education. This convergence of education with religion is best exemplified among Defoe's novels in *Colonel Jacque* where the hero of the novel, bemoaning his early neglect of education says:

I was, . . ., above 30 year old, and had gone thro' some Variety in the World; but as I was perfectly abandoned in my Infancy, and utterly without Instruction in my Youth; so I was entirely ignorant of everything that was worthy the name of Religion. . . .[34]

At this point in his 'post entry' progress in education Colonel Jacque told his tutor to leave off teaching him Latin and teach him religion.

It has already been seen how Defoe attacked Oxford and Cambridge for their tendency towards immorality through the showing of plays which led to religion's being held up to ridicule. His advocacy of compatibility between students' religion, studies and leisure, while at university, was in keeping with his tenet of the need for religion in education *throughout* their lives. Like the Jesuits, Defoe believed in an early start to a Christian education.[35] In an amusing early dialogue of *The Family Instructor* (1718) he advised on the reading of the Bible for the further acquisition of Christian knowledge. Defoe wrote:

I would recommend earnestly to you, the Reading of the Scriptures, and searching for the Meaning and Coherence of every Thing, one with another. Study them, as well as read them; and as they are a Treasure of Wisdom and heavenly Knowledge, you will encrease apace in Knowledge and Experience.[36]

It is in his *New Family Instructor* (1727), however, that Defoe made his most concerted effort to promote Christian education. He used the instance of an apothecary's family as an "example of a sober, well-taught, and religiously educated family," In doing so, Defoe outlined a plan for the progressive acquisition of a Christian education beginning with twice daily readings from the Bible and daily post-prandial religious discourse, suitable to the understanding of young children. Further, Defoe declared that "Religious Instruction is never at an End, till our Children cease to be Children."[37]

Correction and Punishment

One of the more salient features of the Christian religion is the doctrine of original sin. This doctrine has been at the base of pedagogic discipline since time immemorial.[38] According to the doctrine, children have within them the potential for much evil or mischief which must be transmuted through a process of corporal punishment into a nature with a potential for good. Thus the curse of Adam, the result of the Fall, was to be beaten out of children and replaced to a certain extent by pleasing behaviour. If the rod were to be spared, then the child would be spoiled.

Harsh pedagogic practice, even before the doctrine of original sin, had been the orthodoxy for centuries, Quintilian being one of the earliest exceptions among practising schoolmasters. Dr. Richard Busby, a contemporary of Defoe and Headmaster of Westminster School from 1638 to 1695, was a proverbial wielder of the birch. Defoe would be well aware of this most famous London schoolmaster who maintained the discipline of his school for fifty-nine years through his effective use of the birch. Defoe, in some ways, is orthodox in his views on corporal punishment. He accepted the doctrine of original sin when he averred in *The Family Instructor*, Vol. 1, that

> a natural Propensity we all have to evil; with this we are all born into the World, the Soul is originally bent to *Folly*; this Bent or Inclination must be rectified or *driven out* either by *Instruction*, or if that proves insufficient, by *Correction*, and it is to be done while the Person is *young*, while he is a *child* and then IT MAY be done. (Defoe's italics) [39]

The need for early correction is stressed by Defoe and supported scripturally by reference to Solomon who in his wisdom had declared that "Folly, bound up in the Heart of a Child is driven thence by the *Rod of Correction*." Defoe warned that correction or punishment at a later stage has the undesirable effect of causing resentment and friction between children and their parents.

Having established the need for early correction of children in volume one of *The Family Instructor*, Defoe gave sound advice in the second volume on how punishment should be inflicted. In the preface to this volume Defoe expostulated:

> Correction! the most necessary Part of the Family-Government, and the best Part of Education, how difficult a Thing is it! How little understood! How generally wrong applyed! Omitted in necessary and administered in unnecessary Cases! The Nature, Reason, and End of it mistaken! The Measure of it taken not from the Circumstances of the Childrens offences, but from our own Tempers at that Time! [40]

Defoe endeavoured to give advice on these several points raised in the preface and in doing so he stressed the need for parents *not* to punish in the heat of anger. To beat a child or a horse mercilessly is only to store up trouble for the future. In the process of corporal punishment, according to Defoe, it should be explained to the child why punishment was being administered. He wrote:

> Blows are to be given for Instruction; if you give your Child Correction without Reproof and Perswasion, you do like a careless Physician, that sends you Physick, but gives no Direction when, or how to take it. [41]

He advised that

> Pity, not Passion, should influence you in the Conduct of your Child; and a sincere Zeal for his Soul's Good, should be the only Motive of Correction.[42]

In this manner he inveighed against the role of anger in the process of punishment, which was to be tempered by love, pity, duty and zeal for good.

Defoe expressed similar sentiments in his *Religious Courtship* (1722) when in a dialogue between a brother and sister he expounded the view that "there is no Case in the World, that can possibly happen, which ought to make a Father act in a Passion with his own Children."[43] A father who punished fairly, according to Defoe "should have the Rod in his Hand, and Tears in his Eyes; he is to be angry at their Offences, but not with their Persons."[44]

It has already been noted[45] that Defoe appeared to be cantankerous in his old age towards the young. In the two pamphlets in which he accused at least some of the rising generation of ingratitude, *The Protestant Monastery* (1726) and *Chickens Feed Capons* (1731), Defoe was less than liberal in his advice on the treatment of the young. In both *The Protestant Monastery* and *Chickens Feed Capons* he invoked the dictum 'Spare the rod and spoil the child' and criticized those parents who encourage their children to despise their tutors. He affirmed that "as Youth are committed to their Care, so they ought to be subject to their Discipline."[46] If this discipline were not imposed then, said Defoe, adults deserve all they get in contempt and insolence from the young.

It is possible to argue a case for consistency in Defoe's attitudes to punishment over the years insofar as he had a belief in a strict but just and fair policy towards the correction of the young. Where change is detectable perhaps is in the varying emphases he gave to it. In his earlier works he is anxious lest the child be crushed by the burden of a punishment administered in anger; in his later works he is more concerned with the efficacy of punishment in eradicating original sin, the degree of which efficacy would have some bearing on the comfort of one's own declining years.

Teaching and Learning

It has been seen in the preceding section that the second volume of Defoe's *The Family Instructor* is the work in which he expounded, at greatest length and depth, his views on correction and punishment. At one stage in that work he analyzed correction as having three parts: Reproof, Instruction, and Punishment.[47] Defoe was, in fact, using the term rather loosely since he went on to define instruction as "no more or less than an Exhortation, which

72

the Parent should always give the Child to reform."[48] It is more usual to regard correction as an adjunct to instruction rather than view instruction as being subsumed by correction. Despite this seeming confusion Defoe has much to say on the elements of instruction: the complementary processes of teaching and learning; and his observations can be interpreted as educational principles. It will be necessary, however, in view of the discursive nature of these observations, to examine no less than five of his major works and some minor works in order to elicit fully his ideas on teaching and learning.

Rousseau indicated the educational value of *Robinson Crusoe* to a world already familiar with its story of perilous shipwreck, prolonged isolation and eventual rescue. In doing so he affirmed it would furnish Émile with material, both for work and play. He declared

> His head should be full of it, he should always be busy with his castle, his goats, his plantations. Let him learn in detail, not from books but from things, all that is necessary.[49]

In short, Rousseau acclaimed Defoe's first novel as the universal model of learning by doing. In his desert wilderness, Crusoe had found himself applying to the task of survival skills which he did not know he possessed. He found himself able to handle tools; to make necessary furniture and develop a sturdy practical independence, which in civilized society, there had been less need to establish. Such a tale as *Robinson Crusoe* was based on a sense-realist approach to knowledge. As Defoe wrote ten years later, in his *The Compleat English Gentleman*, "the knowledge of things, not words, make a schollar."[50]

It is a truism that beliefs are forged upon the anvil of experience. Similarly educational beliefs or tenets are formed partly, if not largely or wholly, through experience as either a learner or teacher. Even in instances where this does not seem to be the case, where individuals are no longer learners and have not become pedagogues, yet pontificate on the process of instruction, it is likely that such views rest upon experiences in the distant past, when instruction was perhaps the major part of their daily experience. To pontificate otherwise would seem to be foolish since such views would be based more on prejudice than on practice. Defoe's views were, no doubt, based on his early experiences at Dr. Morton's Academy in Newington Green. Often in his writings Defoe alluded to this distinguished scholar who, as previously indicated, eventually became Vice-President of Harvard University in Cambridge, Massachusetts.

Defoe, in *The Compleat English Gentleman*, referred, as already noted, to "a tutor of unquestioned reputation for learning"[51] who set up an English academy as a reaction to the then current practice of concentrating on study of Latin and Greek which resulted in the neglect of other subjects since little time was left for anything else. Defoe shared this view which was to form the basis for his proposals for the study of the Classics in the vernacular by his gentlemanly 'post entries.' At Newington Green, if Morton were indeed the "tutor of unquestioned reputation for learning," modern subjects, like Physics, Astronomy, Geography, History and English, were taught successfully. Defoe was even more explicit about the two types of learning, when writing in *Applebee's Journal* in 1725: according to William Lee, Defoe was writing about his own education, comparing it with others. He referred there to a man (perhaps himself) "who could speak five languages, and could read six, who was a master of science, who discoursed of the stars and the regions above, as if he had been born there, who had the history of the world all in his head, the geography of it at his finger's ends, and understood the interests of all nations as if he had lived among them" yet was not considered a scholar or man of learning.[52] By comparison, he went on to attack the learning of a Cambridge don, when he observed,

> he knows Letters, and perhaps could read half the Polyglot Bible but knows nothing of the World,—has neither read Men nor Things; and this, they say, is a Scholar.[53]

Certainly Defoe was an intellectual outcast among the writers of the Augustan world, not being a graduate of a university. He was a dunce from Grub Street[54] whose unscholarly pen, as already noted, was entirely despised by Swift, and partially by Pope. It is no wonder that Defoe was occasionally vituperative against those who assumed such academic superiority over his own learning. But if Defoe were not of the University of Oxford, he *was* of the university of life: *Experientia docet* was a guiding principle for him. If his knowledge of the Classics were not as deep as it might be, his knowledge of the world was profound. It is not surprising, therefore, that he underestimated the value of the one, and stressed the value of the other. Yet, he was sensible of the value of books in the vernacular, as is evidenced in *The Compleat English Gentleman*, when he affirmed their worth as vicarious experiences in fields of study like History or Geography.[55] Defoe's own educational experience, as has been suggested, was probably the basis of his ideas on learning and teaching.

Unlike his famous admirer, Rousseau, who advocated a reversal of all the traditional practice if the correct methods were to be achieved and accordingly recommended a negative education for Émile until the age of twelve, Defoe was in favour of as early a start as possible to formal education. For him the task was simply that of inducing the child to accept the need for learning. As he wrote in *The Family Instructor*, Vol. 1, the difficulty in early education

> does not lie so much in the Question what to teach them . . . as to bring them by Reasoning and Argument to be *teachable*, to persuade them that they have any Occasion to learn or that any are capable of teaching them, and to cause them to *submit* to Instruction in general.[56]

The sentiment is re-echoed in his *New Family Instructor* (1727) when he averred that "'Tis one of the worst Parts of Folly, when Children think they need no Teaching."[57]

In view of the close links between the concepts of learning and nature, insofar as a study of the learning process leads to a study of the psychological background or natural endowment of the pupil, it is not surprising to discover that Defoe's interest in Peter the Wild Boy in *Mere Nature Delineated* led him to consider the process of learning, however superficially. Defoe raised some very perceptive questions about the learning process of the deaf and dumb when he pondered on the difficulties involved in conceptualization in the absence of vocabulary since, as he noted, "Words are to us, the Medium of Thought; we cannot conceive of Things, but by their Names. . . ."[58] In his consideration of the learning process, he acutely observed that the learner was not discriminating in what was learned and that there was, therefore, a need for guidance in the learning process. The recognition of the undeveloped state of the wild boy's mind led Defoe to dwell on elements involved in this learning process. He based his ideas on those of faculty psychology, recognizing the importance of the faculty of memory in learning.[59] Without memory there would be no speech. 'Meaning,' was another concept which Defoe associated with learning since it was necessary for articulations to have meaning. This consideration of the faculties associated with learning led Defoe to consider the logical steps involved in building up a programme of learning activities. He considered the learning of the skills of reading, writing, and computation and the study of religion—the rudiments of learning for the lower orders—in a progression of stages of learning. Generally, therefore, Defoe was traditional in his outlook, desiring an early start to formal education, and the acquisition of basic skills.

On the obverse side of the instructional coin Defoe considered the pedagogical skill of imparting knowledge. In his *New Family Instructor*, Defoe caused his apothecary-father (probably modelled on his own self-concept) to instruct his children so that instruction became a pleasure to the children by ensuring that the level of instruction was appropriate and within the bounds of their understanding. The interest that he engendered in their studies was increased by making the studies varied within the limits of a wide curriculum.

Defoe considered curriculum on a more grandiose scale in *The Compleat English Gentleman* where he examined what subjects should be self-taught by the 'post entry' gentleman who was attempting to make up leeway in his education. Geography, astronomy, various branches of natural philosophy, English, history and foreign languages formed Defoe's projected curriculum. Such a curriculum was similar to the one Defoe experienced himself at Newington Green.

Although Defoe strongly appreciated the beneficial effects of applying Art to Nature, which interaction could be interpreted as the pedagogic process, he quite often showed ambivalent feeling towards teachers themselves. In *Mere Nature Delineated* he was quite clear as to the importance of the teacher in the learning process. He wrote,

> as he [the pupil] can neither speak, read, write, dance, swim, fence or perform some of the best and most necessary Actions in Life without being taught, so neither can he know, think, retain, judge, discern, distinguish, determine ... without the Guidance of an Instructor; I mean, without being at first led into these Things by the Hand of Teacher ... the first Introduction must be by the Help of Instruction.[60]

In the light of Defoe's high estimation of the value of instruction it is not surprising that he should show some concern in *The Protestant Monastery* for the loss of stature experienced by some private tutors who, being put on the same footing as servants, were prevented from teaching "in a manner suitable to the Dignity of an Instructor."[61] Defoe, looking at contemporary schools, saw there also a diminution of the school teachers' authority. He gave a valuable glimpse into eighteenth-century private schools when he observed,

> Nothing [is] more common nowadays, than for Parents to make it in their Bargain, that their Children shall not be whipt, or otherwise corrected at School. Hence proceeds all that Noise and Misrule, which reigns in Schools, stunning both Master and Scholars to such a Degree, that they can hardly hear each other speak.[62]

Despite these sympathetic observations about the lot of both the private tutor and the public school-master, Defoe is capable of contempt for the school teacher, especially the mere pedant, and the private tutor. Defoe had hinted at criticism of governesses put in charge of young children, when in *The Family Instructor*, Vol. 2, he referred to possible animosity between them and the children. Although Defoe was not generalizing in this instance, when he caused the children in his paradigm to refer to their governess as 'the House-tyrant,' he was more specific and direct in *The Compleat English Gentleman* when he referred to tutors as "those murtherers of a child's moralls."[63] Further he had no more respect for schoolmasters whom he likened to tradesmen dealing "in words and syllables as haberdashers deal in small ware."[64]

Tradesmen's Education and the Practical

Perhaps Defoe's most idiosyncratic contributions to educational thought are his ideas on the education of tradesmen. Writing from his vast experience in trade and commerce he was able to comment with confidence on what was required educationally to make successful tradesmen. Adopting an Aristotelian golden mean between a dunce and a scholar, Defoe was of the opinion that a tradesman's education should be sufficient to make for success in a world of business, and no more. Such an education was, in essence, a modest one. Defoe expressed this view of desiderata for a tradesman's education in *Colonel Jacque* where the hero was made to observe,

> However, in Half a Years time, or thereabouts; I could Read and Write too tollerably well, in so much that I began to think I was now fit for business.[65]

Mastery of the three R's, some bookkeeping and a fund of commonsense were all that a business or tradesman needed, to achieve success. Defoe wrote,

> The tradesman should be wise rather than witty; he should be as wise as he can in his business; and though he passes for nobody among the Beaus, and wits of town, Nature's weathercocks, ... he will be some body in his own way, and build upon a foundation that his posterity may have room to value themselves upon; and if he cannot be a gentleman, he may be able to buy a gentleman, and thats enough to him.

He went on,

> Business is a Thing suited to a staid Head; it does not require the polite Part of human Understanding, or call for a liberal Education; and it is the Tradesman's Mercy that this is so: But at the same Time, he knows little of Business who thinks a Tradesman may be a Fool, an Idiot or a Natural.[66]

Complementary to Defoe's idea of the future tradesmen's need for only a modest education was the conviction of their social mobility. Unlike tradesmen in France, English tradesmen were able to rise socially and join the ranks of the gentry and even of the aristocracy. Defoe reminded his readers that, *inter alia*, the then late Earl of Haversham (Sir John Thompson, 1647-1710) was originally a merchant; the then late James Craggs (1657-1721) postmaster-general, had been the son of a barber; and that the great grandfather of the then Duke of Bedford had also been a tradesman.[67] One is reminded of Defoe himself when he refers to

> the tradesmen of England, as they grow wealthy, coming every day to the Herald's office, to search for the Coats of Arms of their ancestors in order to paint them on their coaches.[68]

All these tradesmen had one thing in common: their knowledge, rather than of books, was of the world, which Defoe regarded as the best education.

Defoe and Travel

A major lacuna in Defoe's treatment of the education of a gentleman is its almost total lack of reference to travel as part of the education of a gentleman. Defoe made one brief comment on the value or rather lack of value of travel which would have done credit to Bishop Richard Hurd (1720-1808) who in his *Uses of Foreign Travel* showed himself to be the chief critic of travel in the eighteenth century as part of a young gentleman's education. It would seem that Defoe, despite his own extensive travelling both in the British Isles and in Europe and despite his three volumed *Tour through the Island of Great Britain,* did not consider travel to be a necessary part of education, even for a gentleman. It is possible, however, that Defoe had planned to say something on travel in his unfinished book.

In the *New Family Instructor,* for example, he regarded a sound religious education as a *sine qua non* before travelling on the continent and before being laid open to the snares of the world. In this Defoe would seem to be paradoxical. Knowledge of the world, he avers, is the best education yet he does not seem keen to propound the virtues of travel as an educational experience. Perhaps Defoe was unable to escape from his own educational experience which was not gentlemanly in character: perhaps, on the other hand, he was only too much aware of the dangers, both physical and moral, of travel in the eighteenth century. Whatever the reasons, Defoe seems paradoxically reticent in recommending travel as an educational medium.

Summary

It has been my purpose in this chapter to examine the educational ideas of Daniel Defoe which lay behind the attitudes evinced in his writings. The line between beliefs, ideas or tenets and criticism and advice outlined in previous chapters is a difficult one to draw, but the former are the mainsprings for the latter. In sum, Defoe has been seen as having great faith in the beneficial effects of education on mere nature, but realizing at the same time that limitations of those effects are imposed by nature. He believed in the value of an early start to education when the child is still malleable and responsive to parental influences. The bond between parents and children was to be close in order to maximize these influences, although clearly his own attitudes towards some of the young, at least, were modified over the years. The family was an important factor in promoting education, which view was partly influenced by the desultory persecution of the dissenters. Throughout his writings, Defoe was a champion of women's education, and saw in its neglect a waste of nature. As a devout, if worldly, dissenter, he had a profound belief in a Christian education which was to be given in the family circle at an early age. Defoe's ideas on correction and punishment show him to be a humanitarian, who while seeing the dangers of corporal punishment, recognized its necessity. His views were tempered wih compassion and justice. Although he himself had not been a pedagogue he nevertheless showed great interest in the learning and teaching aspects of education. He asked some fairly fundamental questions about how learning takes place even if he were not able to offer any answers. His attitude towards teaching and teachers was consistent with his attitude to education generally, although some pedagogues, both tutors and teachers, earned his hostility by their perversion of education. The emphasis Defoe gives to the education of tradesmen separates him from the Lockean tradition of gentlemanly education. Such then were the basic ideas and attitudes toward education of Defoe. I will try to assess his contribution to educational thought.

CHAPTER 6

Defoe as Educationist: An Assessment

Pope, the arbiter of contemporary eighteenth-century literary taste, observed that, "Defoe wrote a vast many things; and none bad, though none excellent. ... There is something good in all he has written."[1] His writings on education, forming part of that output, were varied in quality and occurred throughout his literary career. Any attempt to assess the value of Defoe as an educationist must take into account the differing contexts of the eighteenth and twentieth centuries. The varying *Weltanschauungen* of eighteenth-century England differed, in many contrasting ways, from twentieth-century Britain, not least in thinking about education. The emphasis given to the development of intellectual powers in the twentieth century would seem strange to Defoe who, although aware of its importance, nevertheless gave emphasis in his writings to other aspects, especially the moral and the religious. This is one of the difficulties, as already suggested, involved in a study of an age earlier than the nineteenth century—viz., what constituted education *per se*? Is it possible to distinguish between education writings and courtesy literature, or between educational thoughts and moral didacticism? This problem is brought sharply into focus when the Victorian commentator William Lee eulogizes the didactic worth of Defoe's *Family Instructor*. Lee writes:

> It [*The Family Instructor*] has found its way into the libraries of Kings, and into the cottages of peasants: it has passed through innumerable editions and is still popular; it has been made a blessing, under God, to thousands of souls, and will continue to be the same, wherever the English language is known, and so long as that which is pure and peaceable, shall continue to be lovely, and of good report.[2]

Ignoring the Victorian sanctimony, it is difficult to overlook the point Lee is making, that *The Family Instructor* was a widely adopted and well read book in earlier times. If it is permissible to regard its contents as 'educational' then it would seem Defoe has a powerful claim to being regarded as an acknowledged educational thinker, at least for the eighteenth and nineteenth centuries. To exclude him is to be guilty of another 'Whig interpretation.'[3]

Heavily laden with religion though *The Family Instructor* may be, it never-theless reflects contemporary notions on education. Lee reinforces this view when, alluding to the second volume of *The Family Instructor*, he suggests that "there are few books better adapted for the perusal of all to whom the education of the young is committed; the clergy of every denomination,—teachers of National and Sunday Schools, parents, children and servants."[4] Today only the historian of education would look at it for its educational value. Defoe's educational ideas, however, were consistently imbued with religious sentiment and reflected the extent of religious writings in the eight-eenth century. As Michael Shinagel affirmed in *Daniel Defoe and Middle Class Gentility*, religious works were the most popular single category of book throughout the eighteenth century: something like two-hundred religious works were published annually.[5] Defoe was no mean contributor to this out-put.

Another difficulty in considering Defoe's contribution to educational thought is that much of his writing on the subject forms the *obiter dicta* of works devoted to another major subject. It is possible to distil some Defoean educational wisdom from some forty of his works, if his novels are admissible as reflectors of educational attitudes. The researcher of Defoe, has, therefore, to spread the net widely in order to ensure a comprehensive survey. Discur-sive though Defoe may appear at first sight to be in his educational thinking, it is possible to discern (a) that most of his educational writing occurs after 1714 and (b) that some of his key educational ideas can be identified with one book. In the light of the second observation, it can be seen that his ideas on correction and punishment are to be found in the second volume of *The Family Instructor*; his ideas on a liberal education in *The Compleat English Gentleman*; his ideas on the learning process and 'nature' in *Mere Nature Delineated*; and his ideas on youthful obedience in *The Protestant Monas-tery*. His exploratory thoughts on Language are to be found in *An Essay upon Projects* and *The Compleat English Gentleman*; his ideas on moral education in *The Family Instructor* and *Religious Courtship*; and his ideas on practical education in the two volumes of the *Complete English Trades-man* and (on the authority of Rousseau) in *Robinson Crusoe*. Finally his educational projects are to be found principally in his *An Essay upon Proj-ects* and *Augusta Triumphans*.

Some of Defoe's ideas are pertinent only to the times in which he lived. His concern for the education of Dissenters, for example, reflects contempor-ary concern for sectarian persecution. Because of the 'temporal' nature of these, such ideas as he had about eighteenth-century dissenting education can be regarded as being only 'pragmatic' in character. Others, like his views

81

on the desirability of early education or a liberal education partly through scientific study and using the vernacular can be said to be 'transcendental' insofar as they transcend their context and can be considered freed from it. Accepting then this possible division of his ideas as a paradigm, it is possible to discern three levels of value in his educational thinking. First, he has value as a commentator on the contemporary scene and for this reason historians of education concerned with either charity schools or dissenting academies in the eighteenth century ought to consult Defoe. Secondly, his 'pragmatic' ideas on education, such as those influenced by his Puritan religious sentiments, partly reflect his eighteenth-century *Weltanschauung*. Finally, his ideas which transcend the eighteenth century, entitle him to consideration as an educational thinker in his own right.

Defoe was a 'modern' who, in *The Compleat English Gentleman*, was critical of the barren methods of learning the classics both in the universities and the schools. His own proposals for a 'post entry' liberal education dispensed with the burden of memorizing. His advocacy of the vernacular offered a route to learning which made the most economical use of limited time, while his support for a wider curriculum, taking in, *inter alia*, science and the use of globes, showed him to be a sense-realist at a time when Baconians were still in a minority. As Shinagel has observed,

> In proposing these basic educational reforms he [Defoe] was not unique, although his position ranked him among the few truly enlightened theorists of the age.[6]

Defoe was a 'modern' in education as well as a man of the future in other fields—a great educational projector in an age of projection.

In trying to assess Defoe as an educationist, it becomes necessary to ask to what extent did he strive to be overtly that? Any examination of his busy life must lead to the conclusion that Defoe was mainly concerned with other spheres of activity: with politics, trade, religion, and commerce *before* education.[7] Further, his writings outside education were so prolific that it becomes difficult to establish a case for his quiet and serious consideration of education *per se*, although clearly his *The Family Instructor, Of Royall Educacion, Complete English Tradesman* and the *Compleat English Gentleman* give the lie to that thought. He seemed always to be in a hurry. Between 1704 and 1713, for instance, he wrote his *Review* consisting of 5,000 pages during which time he wrote also some eighty other works containing 4,727 pages. This prodigious effort becomes all the more astonishing when it is recalled that for five years simultaneously he was engaged, first by Harley and then by Godolphin, as political agent among the Scots.

Certainly Defoe is wider than Locke in his consideration of education; more consistent than is Rousseau but also less rigorous in his thinking because of the journalistic pace of his existence. His educational writings, however, do not have the depth of either Locke or Rousseau. One possible test of his authenticity as an influential educator would be an assessment of the extent he is quoted by others as an authority on education. Apart from Rousseau, who in any case praises *Robinson Crusoe* rather than Daniel Defoe, there is little reference, if any, by others to his educational ideas. In education, as in life, Defoe remains an enigma; he was not so much an educationist as a quasi-educationist, a man who wrote much on the subject of education but whom posterity has ignored, at least to date, as a source of educational wisdom.

NOTES

NOTES TO CHAPTER I

[1] M. Henry, and Emmie Felkin, *An introduction to Herbart's Science and Practice of Education*, Swan Sonnenschein and Co., 1901, p. 130. Tuiskon Ziller (1817-1882) was one of the leading neo-Herbartians who, after Herbart's death in 1841, set out to perpetuate his principles in education.

[2] J. J. Rousseau, *Emile*, Everyman edition, 1974, p. 147.

[3] John R. Moore in "Robinson Crusoe" in Frank H. Ellis (Ed.), *Twentieth Century Interpretations of Robinson Crusoe*, Prentice-Hall, 1969, p. 56.

[4] *Ibid.*, p. 56.

[5] *Op. cit.*, 1783, pp. 566-7 as quoted in Pat Rogers (Ed.), *Defoe—the Critical Heritage*, Routledge and Kegan Paul, 1972, p. 59.

[6] Lecture XXVII Blair's, *Lectures on Rhetoric and Belles Lettres*, 1783, as quoted in Walter Wilson, *Memoirs of the Life and Times of Daniel Defoe* (London) 1830, p. 60.

[7] Wilson, *op. cit.*, p. 60.

[8] Sir Leslie Stephen, *Hours in a Library*, Vol. 1, Smith, Elder and Co., 1907, p. 54. Quoted also by Pat Rogers, *op. cit.*, p. 175.

[9] George Borrow, *Lavengro*, John Murray, 1851, p. 19.

[10] Sir Walter Besant, *Autobiography*, Hutchinson, 1902, p. 48. His first readings were *Robinson Crusoe*, *Pilgrim's Progress* and the *Book of Revelation*.

[11] J. S. Mill, *Autobiography*, with a foreword by Asa Briggs, a Signet Classic, New American Library, 1964.

[12] Daniel Defoe, *The Life and Strange Surprizing Adventures of Robinson Crusoe*, Studley Press, 1947, p. 60.

[13] *Ibid.*, p. 173.

[14] *Ibid.*, p. 62.

[15] H. Maclachlan, *English Education under the Test Acts*, Manchester University Press, 1931.

[16] Irene Parker, *Dissenting Academies in England*, Cambridge University Press, 1914.

[17] J. W. Ashley Smith, *The Birth of Modern Education*, Independent Press, 1954.

[18] Unpublished manuscript by co-authors Dr. D. P. Leinster-Mackay and Dr. John Hay, University of Western Australia.

[19] Francis Watson, *Daniel Defoe*, Longmans, Green and Co., 1952, Chapter 4. The term 'polygrapher' was used earlier by George Saintsbury in his *The Peace of the Augustans*, G. Bell and Sons, 1916, p. 108.

NOTES TO CHAPTER 2

[1] Cf. G. M. Trevelyan, *English Social History*, Longmans Green and Co., 1947, Chapter X.

[2] Defoe, being concerned about the need for a smooth succession by the House of Hanover used irony in his pamphleteering as he had done earlier with *The Shortest Way with the Dissenters* and in so doing was misunderstood once again and arrested. Compare *Whigs Turn'd Tories* (1713) and *A Letter to the Whigs* (1714).

[3] Cf. Basil Williams, *The Whig Supremacy*, 1714-1760, Oxford University Press, 1952.

[4] Henry St. John, Viscount Bolingbroke (1678-1751), author of the *Patriot King*, aided the Jacobite cause in 1715 but later made his peace with Robert Walpole.

[5] Simon Aleyn who lived during the reigns of Charles I, Charles II, James II, William and Mary, Anne, George I, and the Interregnum, as Vicar of the Parish of Bray in Berkshire and changed his loyalties when it was expedient to do so.

[6] Viz., James II, William III, Queen Anne, and George I. Cf. John R. Moore, *Daniel Defoe: Citizen of the Modern World*, p. 202.

[7] John Tutchin in his *Observator* attacked Defoe on this account, as did Dr. Browne in his *The Review Reviewed* (May 1705). Defoe attacked Mr. Observator and Dr. B. for their slur on his person, in *The Review* Vol. II, pp. 149-50.

[8] Defoe, *op. cit.*, 1725, p. 376. Cf. also *The Little Review*, pp. 46-47.

[9] Cf. J. H. Parry, *Europe and a Wider World 1415-1715*, Hutchinson's University Library, 1949, for account of early English colonial empire. Chapters VII and IX.

[10] Cf. *Giving Alms no Charity* (1704); *Charity Still a Christian Virtue* (1719); *Parochial Tyranny* (1727).

[11] Cf. pp. 57-58.

[12] For an interesting discussion on the prevailing characteristics of contemporary literary and aesthetic criticism see Donald Greene, *The Age of Exuberance*, Random House, 1970, pp. 159-62.

[13] I.e., writers who acknowledged their debt to authors like Horace and Virgil, of the Augustan Age in the first century, B.C.

[14] Defoe, *op. cit.*, pp. 230-31.

[15] Cf. Pat Rogers, *Grub Street: Studies in a Subculture*, Methuen, 1972, pp. 1-17, pp. 311-27.

[16] Alexander Pope, *The Dunciad* Book 2, Everymans Library, J. M. Dent and Sons, 1949, p. 140, ll. 147-48. Pope inaccurately refers to Defoe's ignominy of being pilloried, a punishment which was as dishonourable as that meted out to John Tutchin, editor of *The Observator*, who was sentenced to be whipped.

[17] *Review* 1709, Vol. VI, p. 220.

[18] *Ibid.*, Vol. III, 8th August 1706, pp. 377-80; 10th August 1706, pp. 381-83.

[19] *Ibid.*, Vol. IV, 2nd October 1707, p. 397.

[20] Cf. p. 22.

[21] Cf. W. K. Lowther-Clarke, *A history of the S.P.C.K.*, S.P.C.K., 1959.

[22] Cf. Christopher Wordsworth, *Scholae Academicae*, Frank Cass. 1968.

[23] For years jubilant Jacobites toasted 'the little gentleman in black velvet.'

[24] Cf. James Sutherland, *Defoe* 1937, p. 89.

[25] Cf. G. M. Trevelyan, *England Under Queen Anne: Blenheim*, Fontana Library, 1965, p. 348.

[26] *Op. cit.*, Vol. V, 20th November 1708, p. 407; *Ibid.*, Vol. VI, 5th August 1709, pp. 11-12.

[27] Cf. George H. Healey, *The Letters of Daniel Defoe*, Oxford University Press, 1955, pp. 450-54.

[28] E.g., James Sutherland, *Defoe*, Methuen, 1937, pp. 211-13.

[29] Cf. B. G. Ivanyi article in the *Times Literary Supplement*, 7th April 1966.

[30] There are some doubts as to whether or not Defoe was responsible for this. It has been credited to a William Bond insofar as that name appears with the new title *The Supernatural Philosopher* in 1728. It is possible, however, that Defoe used William Bond as yet another alias. Rodney M. Baine questions the ascription to Defoe of both *Duncan Campbell* and *The Dumb Philosopher* in *Daniel Defoe and the Supernatural*, University of Georgia Press, 1968, chapters 7 and 8.

NOTES TO CHAPTER 3

[1] Defoe, *op. cit.*, pp. 300-01.

[2] It is quite likely that this school was the village school at Martock where a relative of Defoe was the school-master, cf. Daniel Defoe, *A Tour through the whole island of Great Britain*, Penguin English Library, p. 216. This verse, modified, appears also at the end of Chapter 1 in Defoe's *Of Royall Educacion* (1895), an unfinished work.

[3] Defoe, *op. cit.*, p. 122.

[4] Defoe, *op. cit.*, p. 282.

[5] *A Review of the Affairs of France*, Vol. 1, p. 156, 1704.

[6] *A Review of the State of the British Nation*, Vol. VI, p. 220, 1709.

[7] *Ibid.*, Vol. III, p. 377.

[8] *Ibid.*, p. 379.

[9] *Ibid.*, p. 378.

[10] *Ibid.*, 10th August 1706, p. 381.

[11] *A Review of the State of the British Nation*, Vol. IV, 2nd October 1707, p. 397.

[12] The use of the term 'Publick School' by Defoe is of interest to the historian of education concerned with the alleged evolution of this term from 'Great School' in the *late* eighteenth century.

[13] D. Defoe, *The Compleat English Gentleman*, pp. 7-8.

[14] William Lee, *Daniel Defoe: His Life and Recently Discovered Writings* (3 Vols.) London: 1869, Vol. II, pp. 301-02.

[15] Defoe, *The Present State of the Parties in Great Britain*, p. 298.

[16] *Ibid.*, p. 299.

[17] George H. Healey (Ed.), *Letters of Daniel Defoe*, Oxford University Press, 1955, Letter 225, p. 440.

[18] D. Defoe, *The Present State of the Parties in Great Britain*, p. 316.

[19] *Ibid.*, p. 317.

[20] *Ibid.*, p. 318.

[21] *The Compleat English Gentleman*, Ed., K. Bulbring, 1895, p. 14.

[22] *Ibid.*, p. 35.

[23] Quoted by George C. Brauer, *The Education of a Gentleman: Theories of Gentlemanly Education in England 1660-1775*, New York: 1959, p. 16.

[24] *Ibid.*, p. 16.

[25] *The Compleat English Gentleman*, p. 69.

[26] *Ibid.*, p. 70.

[27] *Ibid.*, p. 180.

[28] *Ibid.*, p. 116.

[29] *Ibid.*, p. 87.

NOTES TO CHAPTER 4

[1] Defoe, *The Compleat English Gentleman*, p. 145.

[2] *Ibid.*, p. 196.

[3] *Ibid.*, p. 186.

[4] *Ibid.*, p. 229.

[5] Cf. *Ibid.*, p. 188.

[6] *Ibid.*, p. 210.

[7] Cf. *Ibid.*, p. 196.

[8] *Ibid.*, pp. 197-98.

[9] *Ibid.*, p. 198.

[10] *Ibid.*, p. 198.

[11] *Ibid.*, p. 225.

[12] Defoe, *The Compleat English Tradesman*, Vol. 1, p. 25.

[13] *Ibid.*, p. 33.

[14] *Ibid.*, pp. 43-44.

[15] Defoe, *The Complete English Tradesman*, Vol. 2, p. 58.

[16] B. Fitzgerald, *Daniel Defoe—a study in conflict*, Secker and Warburg, 1954, pp. 212-13.

[17] W. H. G. Armytage, *Four Hundred Years of English Education*, Cambridge University Press, 1964, p. 28.

[18] *Reasons for a Royal Visitation* (1717), p. 24.

[19] *Augusta Triumphans* (1728), p. 58.

[20] *Ibid.*, p. 8.

[21] Cf. M. F. Alderson and H. C. Colles (Eds.), *History of St. Michael's College Tenbury*, S.P.C.K., 1943.

[22] Juan Vives (1492-1540), Renaissance educator, also favoured education of women as did Plato.

[23] *A Review of the State of the British Nation*, Vol. V, 1708, pp. 374-75.

[24] *Op. cit.*, p. 110.

[25] Defoe, *More Short Ways with the Dissenters* (1704), p. 7.

[26] *Ibid.*, p. 8.

[27] *A Review of the State of the English Nation*, Vol. III, 16th April 1706, pp. 181-82.

[28] Defoe, *The Present State of the Parties in Great Britain* (1712), p. 295.

[29] *Ibid.*, pp. 335-36.

[30] *Ibid.*, pp. 339-41.

[31] *Wise as Serpents* (1712), p. 18.

[32] Defoe, *op. cit.*, Vol. III, 4th March 1712, pp. 594-95.

[33] George H. Healey, *op cit.*, Letters 225 and 226, pp. 439-42.

[34] Cf. G. N. Clark, *The Later Stuarts 1660-1714*, Oxford University Press, 1949, p. 152.

[35] *The Compleat English Gentleman*, p. 218.

[36] William Lee, *op. cit.*, Vol. III, Letters on 6th July and 13th July 1723, pp. 154-59.

[1] Defoe, *op. cit.*, p. 283.

[2] *Ibid.*, p. 260.

[3] Sir Henry Wotton, *A Philosophical Survey of Education or Moral Architecture* (1673), University Press of Liverpool, 1938.

[4] Defoe, *Mere Nature Delineated*, p. 17.

[5] *Ibid.*, p. 63.

[6] Defoe, *The Compleat English Gentleman*, p. 55.

[7] *Ibid.*, p. 108.

[8] *Ibid.*, p. 109.

[9] Daniel Defoe, *Moll Flanders*, Pan Books, 1965, p. 33.

[10] *The Compleat English Gentleman*, p. 111.

[11] Defoe, *Of Royall Educacion*, p. 4.

[12] Defoe, *op. cit.*, p. 87.

[13] Defoe, *The Family Instructor*, Vol. I, p. 5.

[14] Cf. John R. Moore, *Daniel Defoe: Citizen of the Modern World*, University of Chicago Press, 1958, p. 219.

[15] Cf. George Chalmers, *The Life of Daniel Defoe*, J. Stockdale, London, 1790, p. 51. Francis Watson, *Daniel Defoe*, Longmans, Green and Co., 1952, p. 85.

[16] Cf. John R. Moore, *op. cit.*, p. 218.

[17] Defoe, *Mere Nature Delineated*, pp. 60-61.

[18] Defoe, *The Compleat English Gentleman*, p. 6.

[19] Cf. Defoe, *op. cit.*, p. 66. He suggested that the aim of the book was to write "a satyr upon their neglect of Duty" and to seek parental reform.

[20] Defoe, *The Conduct of Christmas made the Sport of Infidels*, p. 8.

[21] *Ibid.*

[22] Defoe, *The Protestant Monastery*, p. 4.

[23] *Ibid.*, p. 22.

[24] Defoe, *The Compleat English Gentleman*, p. 241.

[25] Cf., p. 33.

[26] Defoe, *The Family Instructor*, Vol. I, p. 63.

[27] Defoe, *The New Family Instructor*, p. iv.

[28] Defoe, *Serious Reflections of Robinson Crusoe*, p. 69.

[29] *Ibid.*, p. 70.

[30] Defoe, *An Essay upon Projects*, p. 304.

[31] *The New Whole Duty of Man*, John Hinton: London, Nineteenth edition, 1763, p. 2.

[32] *Ibid.*, p. 79.

[33] Defoe, *The Life and Surprising Adventures of Robinson Crusoe*, The Studley Press, 1947, p. 130.

[34] Defoe, *Colonel Jacque*, Oxford University Press, 1970, p. 170.

[35] Defoe, *The Family Instructor*, Vol. 1, p. 15.

[36] Defoe, *The Family Instructor*, Vol. 2, pp. 167-68.

[37] Defoe, *The New Family Instructor*, p. 1.

[38] Cf. D. P. Leinster-Mackay, "Regina v Hopley: Some historical reflections on corporal punishment," *Journal of Educational Administration and History*, Vol. IX, No. 1, January 1977, pp. 1-6.

[39] Defoe, *The Family Instructor*, Vol. 1, p. 77.

[40] Defoe, *The Family Instructor*, Vol. 2, p. v.

[41] *Ibid.*, p. 188.

[42] *Ibid.*, p. 191.

[43] Defoe, *Religious Courtship*, p. 110.

[44] *Ibid.*

[45] P. 33.

[46] Defoe, *The Protestant Monastery*, p. 21.

[47] Defoe, *The Family Instructor*, Vol. 2, p. 185.

[48] *Ibid.*

[49] J. J. Rousseau, *Emile*, Everyman's Library, J. M. Dent and Sons 1974, pp. 147-48.

[50] Defoe, *The Compleat English Gentleman*, p. 212.

[51] *Ibid.*, p. 218, cf. p. 64.

[52] William Lee, *op. cit.*, Vol. III, p. 437.

[53] *Ibid.*, p. 439.

[54] Cf. Pat Rogers, *Grub Street: Studies in a Subculture*, Methuen, 1972, Chapter 5.

[55] Defoe, *The Compleat English Gentleman*, p. 226.

[56] Defoe, *The Family Instructor*, Vol. 1, p. 131.

[57] Defoe, *op. cit.*, p. viii.

[58] Defoe, *Mere Nature Delineated*, p. 38.

[59] *Ibid.*, p. 78.

[60] *Ibid.*, p. 62.

[61] Defoe, *The Protestant Monastery*, p. 21.

[62] *Ibid.*, pp. 21-22.

[63] Defoe, *The Compleat English Gentleman*, p. 71.

[64] *Ibid.*, p. 201.

[65] Defoe, *Colonel Jacque*, p. 103.

[66] Defoe, *The Complete English Tradesman*, Vol. II, p. 62.

[67] *The Compleat English Tradesman*, Vol. I, p. 376.

[68] *Ibid.*, p. 377.

NOTES TO CHAPTER 6

[1] J. M. Osborn (Ed.), Joseph Spence, *Observations, Anecdotes, and Characters of Books and Men*, Oxford University Press, Vol. 1, p. 213.

[2] William Lee, *op. cit.*, Vol. 1, p. 248.

[3] Cf. Herbert Butterfield, *The Whig Interpretation of History*, G. Bell and Sons, 1951.

[4] Lee, *op. cit.*, Vol. 1, p. 279.

[5] Michael Shinagel, *op. cit.*, p. 120.

[6] *Ibid.*, p. 236.

[7] Cf. *A Tour through the Whole Island of Great Britain*, Penguin Books, 1971. Although Defoe refers to at least twenty-six educational institutions, ranging from the University of Oxford to Charity Schools, his interest in them appears to be largely topographical. Only once, when he visits the school at Martock, Somerset (p. 216) does he consider educational theory. It could be argued, on the other hand, that a travelogue is not the place for such consideration.

APPENDIX

A List of Defoe's Writings on, or Alluding to, Education

The Character of the Late Dr. Samuel Annesley, By way of Elegy (Folio), 1697.

An Essay upon Projects. Printed by R. R. for Tho. Cockerill, 1697.

More Short Ways with the Dissenters, London, 1704.

A Review of the Affairs of France (including the *Little Review* or an *Inquisition of Scandal*), 1704-1713. (The Review had six different titles during its nine years' existence.)

The Present State of the Parties in Great Britain: Particularly An Enquiry into the State of the Dissenters in England, and the Presbyterians in Scotland; their Religious and Politick Interest consider'd as it respects their Circumstances before and since the late Acts against Occasional Conformity in England, and for Tolleration of Common Prayer in Scotland, London. Printed and sold by J. Baker, 1712.

Wise as Serpents, Being An Enquiry into the Present Circumstances of The Dissenters, And What Measures they ought to take in order to Disappoint the Designs of their Enemies, Prov. xix 25. Smite a Scorner, and the Simple will beware; and reprove one that hath Understanding, and he will understand Knowledge. London, 1712.

The Schism Act Explain'd; Wherein some Methods are laid down how the Dissenters may teach their Schools and Academies as usual, without incurring the Penalties of the said Act. London, 1714.

The Weakest go to the Wall, or the Dissenters Sacrific'd by All Parties: Being A true state of the Dissenters Case, as it respects either High-Church or Low Church. London, 1714.

A Letter to Mr. Steele, occasion'd by his Letter to a Member of Parliament, Concerning The Bill for preventing the Growth of Schism. By a Member of the Church of England. London, 1714.

A brief survey of the legal liberties of the dissenters: And How far the Bill now Depending consists with Preserving the Toleration Inviolably. Wherein the present Bill is Published; and also the Toleration Act at large, that they may be compar'd with one Another. London, 1714.

The Remedy worse than the Disease; or, Reasons against passing the Bill for preventing the Growth of Schism. To which is added a brief Discourse of Toleration and Persecution, Shewing, Their Unavoidable Effects good or bad; and Proving that neither Diversity of Religions, nor Diversity in the Same Religion are Dangerous, much less Inconsistent with good Government. *In a letter to a Noble Earl.* London, J. Baker, 1714.

The Family Instructor: In Three Parts. I Relating to Fathers and Children. II To Masters and Servants. III To Husbands and Wives. By way of Dialogue, With a Recommendatory letter by the Rev. Mr. S. Wright. London, E. Matthews, 1715.

The Quarrel of the Schoolboys at Athens, As lately Acted at a School Near Westminster, 1717.

Reasons for a Royal Visitation: Occasion'd by the Present Great Defection of the Clergy from the Government. Shewing The Absolute Necessity of Purging the Universities, and Restoring Discipline to the Church. Make the Tree good, and the Fruit will be good. Of all the Plagues with which Mankind are curst, ecclesiastick Tyranny's the worst. London, 1717.

The Conduct of Christians made the Sport of Infidels. In a Letter From a Turkish Merchant at Amsterdam To the Grand Mufti at Constantinople: On Occasion of some of our National Follies, but especially the late Scandalous Quarrel among the Clergy, 1717.

The Weekly Journal; or Saturday's Post (Mist's) (Defoe: 1717-1724).

Mr. de la Pillonière's Vindication, Being an Answer to the Two Schoolmasters And Their Boys Tittle Tattle wherein the Dispute between Dr. Snape and Mr. Pillonière is set in a True Light, 1718.

Memoirs of the Life and Eminent Conduct of that Learned and Reverend Divine, Daniel Williams D.D. With some Account of his Scheme, for the Vigorous Propagation of Religion, as well in England as in Scotland, and several other Parts of the World. Address'd to Mr. Peirce, London. Printed for E. Curll, 1718.

The Family Instructor. In Two Parts. I Relating to Family Breaches, and their obstructing Religious Duties. II To the Great Mistake of mixing the Passions, in the Managing and Correcting of Children. With a great Variety of Cases, relating to setting Ill Examples to Children and Servants, Vol. II, 1718.

A Vindication of the Press: Or, An Essay on the Usefulness of Writing, On Criticism, And The Qualification of Authors. Wherein is shewn, That 'tis for the Advantage of all Governments to encourage Writing, otherwise a Nation would never be secure from the Attempts of its most secret Enemies; Barbarous and prejudic'd Criticisms on Writings are detected, and Criticism is justly stated. With an Examination into what Genius's and Learning are necessary for an Author in all manner of performances. London. Printed for T. Warner, 1718.

The Life and Strange Surprizing Adventures of Robinson Crusoe, Of York, Mariner: Who lived Eight and Twenty Years all alone, On an un-inhabited

Island on the Coast of America, near the Mouth of the Great River Oroonoque; Having been Cast on Shore by Shipwreck, wherein all the Men perished but himself. With an Account how he was at last strangely deliver'd by Pyrates. *Written by Himself.* London. Printed for W. Taylor, 1719.

Charity Still a Christian Virtue: Or, An Impartial Account of the Tryal and Conviction of the Reverend Mr. Hendley, For Preaching a Charity-Sermon at Chisselhurst. And of Mr. Campman, Mr. Prat and Mr. Harding, for Collecting at the same Time the Alms of the Congregation. At the Assizes held at Rochester, on Wednesday, July 15, 1719. Humbly offer'd to the Consideration of the Clergy of the Church of England. London. Printed for T. Bickerton, 1719.

Serious Reflections During the Life and Surprizing Adventures of Robinson Crusoe, With his Vision of the Angelick World. Written by Himself. London. Printed for W. Taylor, 1720.

The History of the Life and Adventures of Mr. Duncan Campbell. A Gentleman, who, tho' Deaf and Dumb writes down any Stranger's Name at First Sight; with their future Contingencies of Fortune. Now living in Exeter Court, over against the Savoy in the Strand. London. E. Curll, 1720.

The Life, Adventures, and Pyracies, of the Famous Captain Singleton: Containing an Account of his being set on Shore in the Island of Madagascar, his Settlement there, with a Description of the Place and Inhabitants: Of his Passage from thence, in a Paraguay, to the main Land of Africa, with an Account of the Customs and Manners of the People: His great Deliverance from the barbarous Natives and wild Beasts: Of his meeting with an Englishman, a Citizen of London, among the Indians, the great Riches he acquired, and his Voyage Home to England: As also Captain Singleton's Return to Sea, with an Account of his many Adventures, and Pyracies with the famous Captain Avery and others. London. Printed for J. Brotherton, 1720.

Applebee's Original Weekly Journal. (Defoe: 1720-1726)

The Fortunes and Misfortunes of the Famous Moll Flanders, &c, Who was Born in Newgate, and during a Life of continu'd Variety, for Threescore Years, besides her Childhood, was Twelve Year a Whore, Five Times a Wife (whereof once to her own Brother) Twelve Year a Thief, Eight Year a Transported Felon in Virginia, at last grew Rich, liv'd Honest, and died a Penitent. Written from her own Memorandums. London. W. Chetwood, 1722.

Religious Courtship: Being Historical Discourses on the Necessity of Marrying Religious Husbands and Wives only. As also of Husbands and Wives being of the same Opinions in Religion with one Another. With an Appendix of the Necessity of taking none but Religious Servants, and a Proposal for the better managing of Servants. London. E. Matthews, 1722.

The History and Remarkable Life of the truly Honourable Colonel Jacque, Commonly call'd Col. Jack, Who was born a Gentleman, put 'Prentice to a

Pickpocket, was Six and Twenty Years a Thief, and then Kidnapp'd to Virginia; Came back a Merchant; married four Wives, and five of them prov'd Whores; went into the Wars, behav'd bravely, got Preferment, was made Colonel of a Regiment, came over, and fled with the Chevalier, and is now abroad compleating a Life of Wonders, and resolves to dye a General. London. J. Brotherton, 1722.

The Fortunate Mistress: Or, a History of the Life and Vast Variety of Fortunes of Mademoiselle de Beleau; Afterwards call'd the Countess of Wintselsheim, in Germany. Being the Person known by the Name of the Lady Roxana, in the Time of King Charles II. London. T. Warner, 1724.

The Great Law of Subordination Consider'd; Or, The Insolence; and Unsufferable Behaviour of Servants in England; duly enquir'd into. Illustrated with a great Variety of Examples, Historical cases, and Remarkable Stories of the Behaviour of some particular Servants, suited to all the Several Arguments made us of, as they go on. In Ten Familiar Letters. Together with a Conclusion, being an earnest and Moving Remonstrance to the Housekeepers and Heads of Families in Great Britain, pressing them not to cease using their Utmost Interest (especially at this Juncture), to obtain sufficient Laws, for the effectual Regulation of the Manners and Behaviour of their Servants. As Also A Proposal, containing such Heads, or Constitutions, as wou'd effectually answer this great End, and bring Servants of every Class to a just (and yet not a grievous) Regulation. London. S. Harding, 1724.

A Tour thro' the Whole Island of Great Britain, Divided into Circuits or Journies. Giving A Particular and Diverting Account of Whatever is Curious and worth Observation, Viz: I. A Description of the Principal Cities and Towns, their Situations, Magnitude, Government, and Commerce. II. The Customs, Manners, Speech, as also the Exercises, Diversions, and Employments of the People. III. The Produce and Improvement of the Lands, the Trade, and Manufactures. IV. The Sea Ports and Fortifications with the Course of Rivers, and the Inland Navigation. V. The Publick Edifices, Seats, and Palaces, of the Nobility and Gentry. With Useful Observations upon the Whole. Particularly fitted for the Reading of Such, as desire to Travel over the Island. *By a Gentleman*. London. G. Strahan, 3 vols, 1724-27.

The Complete English Tradesman, In Familiar Letters, Directing him in all the several Parts and Progressions of Trade—viz. I. His acquainting himself with Business during his Apprenticeship. II. His Writing to his Correspondents, and obtaining a general knowledge of Trade, as well what he is not as what he is employ'd in. III. Of Diligence, and Application, as the Life of all Business. IV. Cautious against Over-Trading. V. Of the ordinary Occasions of a Tradesman's Ruin; such as Expensive Living,—Too early Marrying,—Innocent Diversions,—Giving and Taking too much Credit,—Leaving Business to Servants,—Being above Business,—Entering into Dangerous Partnerships &c. VI. Directions in the several Distresses of a Tradesman, when he comes to fail. VII. Of Tradesmen Compounding with their Debtors, and why they are so particularly severe. VIII. Of Tradesmen ruining one another, by Rumour and Scandal. IX. Of the customary Frauds of Trade, which even honest Men allow themselves to practise. X. Of Credit, and how it is only supported by Honesty. XI. Directions for Book-keeping, punctual paying Bills, and thereby maintaining Credit. XII. Of the Dignity and Honour of Trade, in England, more than in other Countries; and how the Trading Families in England are mingled with the Nobility and Gentry, so as not to be separated, or distinguished. Calculated for the Instruction of Our Inland Tradesmen, and especially of Young Beginners. London. Charles Rivington, 1725.

Mere Nature Delineated: Or, A Body without a Soul. Being Observations Upon The Young Forester Lately brought to Town from Germany. With Suitable Applications. Also, A Brief Dissertation upon the Usefulness and Necessity of Fools, whether Political or Natural. London. T. Warner, 1726.

A General History of the Principal Discoveries and Improvements in Useful Arts. Particularly in the Great Branches of Commerce, Navigation, and Plantation in all Parts of the Known World & c. London. J. Roberts, 1726.

The Protestant Monastery: Or, a Complaint Against The Brutality of the Present Age. Particularly the Pertness and Insolence of our Youth to Aged Persons. With a Caution to People in Years how they give the Staff out of their own Hands, and leave themselves to the Mercy of others. Concluding With a Proposal for Erecting a Protestant Monastery, where Persons of small Fortunes may end their Days in Plenty, Ease and Credit, without burthening their Relations, or accepting Publick Charities. By Andrew Moreton Esq. Author of *Everybody's Business is Nobody's Business*. London. W. Meadows, 1726.

The Compleat English Tradesman, Volume II. In two parts. Part I. Directed chiefly to the more Experienced Tradesmen; with Cautions and Advices to them after they are thriven, and suppos'd to be grown rich, viz. I. Against Running out of their Business into needless projects, and Dangerous Adventures, no Tradesman being above Disaster. II. Against oppressing one another by Engrossing, Underselling combinations in Trade &c. III. Advices, that when he leaves off his Business, he should part Friends with the World; the great Advantages of it; with a Word of the Scandalous Character of a Purse-proud Tradesman. IV. Against being litigious and Vexatious, and opt to go to Law for Trifles; with some Reasons why Tradesmen's Differences should if possible all be used by Arbitration. Part II. Being useful Generals in Trade, describing the Principles and Foundations of the Home Trade of Great Britain, with large Tables of our Manufactures, Calculations of the Product, Shipping, Carriage of Goods by hand, Importation from Abroad, Consumption at Home, &c by all which the infinite number of our Tradesmen are employ'd, and the General Wealth of the Nation rais'd and increas'd. The whole calculated for the use of our Inland Tradesmen, as well in the City, as in the Country. London. Printed for Charles Rivington, 1727.

The New Family Instructor: In Familiar Discourses Between a Father and his Children, on the most Essential Points of Christian Religion. In Two

Parts. Part I. Containing a Father's Instructions to his Son upon his going to Travel into Popish Countries; And to the rest of his Children, on his Son's turning Papist; confirming them in the Protestant Religion, against the Absurdities of Popery. Part II. Instructions against the Three Grand Errors of the Times; Viz. 1. Asserting the Divine Authority of the Scriptures; against the Deists. 2. Proofs, that the Messias, is already come &c.; against the Atheists and Jews. 3. Asserting, the Divinity of Jesus Christ, that he was really the same with the Messias, and that the Messias was to be really God; against our Modern Hereticks. With a Poem upon the Divine Nature of Jesus Christ, in Blank Verse. By the Author of the *Family Instructor*. London. T. Warner, 1727.

An Essay on the History and Reality of Apparitions. Being An Account of what they are, and what they are not; whence they come, and whence they come not. As Also How we may distinguish between the Apparitions of Good and Evil Spirits, and how we ought to behave to them. With a great Variety of Surprizing and Diverting Examples, never Publish'd before. By Andrew Moreton Esq., 1727.

Augusta Triumphans: Or, The Way To Make London The most flourishing City in the Universe. I. First, By establishing an University where Gentlemen may have Academical Education under the Eye of their Friends. II. To prevent Murder &c ... by an Hospital for Foundlings. III. By suppressing pretended Mad-Houses, where many of the fair Sex are unjustly confin'd, while their Husbands Keep Mistresses &c and many Widows are lock'd up for the sake of their Jointure. IV. To save our Youth from Destruction, by clearing the Streets of impudent Strumpets, Suppressing Gaming-Tables, and Sunday Debauches. V. To avoid the expensive Importation of Foreign Musicians, by forming an Academy of our own. VI. To save our lower Class of People from utter Ruin, and render them useful, by preventing the immoderate use of Geneva: With a frank explosion of many other common Abuses and incontestable Rules for Amendment. Concluding with an Effectual Method to prevent Street Robberies, And a Letter to Coll. Robinson, on Account of the Orphan's Tax. By Andrew Moreton Esq. London, 1728.

The Supernatural Philosopher: or, the Mysteries of Magick, in all its Branches clearly unfolded, containing. I. An argument proving the Perception, which Mankind have by all the senses of Demons, Genii, or Familiar Spirits; and of the several species of them, both Good and Bad. II. A Philosophical Discourse, concerning the Second sight, demonstrating it to be Hereditary to some families. III. A full Answer to all Objections that can be brought against the existence of Spirits, Witches, &c. IV. Of Divination by Dreams, Omens, Spectres, Apparitions after Death, Predictions &c. V. Of Enchantment, Necromancy, Geomancy, Hydromancy, Aeromancy, Pyromancy, Chiromancy, Augury and Aruspicy. All Exemplified in the History of the Life and Surprizing Adventures of Mr. Duncan Campbell, a Scots Gentleman, who though Deaf and Dumb writes down any stranger's Name at first Sight, with their Future Contingencies of Fortune. Collected and Compiled from the most celebrated Tract written by Dr. Wallis, The Method of

Teaching Deaf and Dumb Persons to read, write, and understand a Language. By William Bond, of Bury St. Edmond's, Suffolk. London. E. Curll. 3rd Edition, 1728.

The Compleat English Gentleman: Containing useful Observations on the general Neglect of the education of English Gentlemen, with the Reason and Remedies. The Apparent Differences between a well born, and a well bred Gentleman. Instructions how Gentlemen may recover a Deficiency of their Latin, and be Men of Learning, though without the Pedantry of Schools. 1729. (Not published till 1890.)

Chickens Feed Capons: Or A Dissertation On The Pertness of our Youth in general, Especially Those trained up at Tea-Tables; With the true Picture of a Petit Maître, and a Modern fine Lady; Some Hints on Abuses in Education; not forgetting the Insolence and Scorn with which the generality of young Persons treat their Elders and Betters. Also a very remarkable Tragical Case, which may serve as a Warning to Persons in Years, how they give the Staff out of their own Hands, and leave themselves to the Mercy of others. Written by a Friend of the Person injured, London. 1731.

The Generous Projector, Or A Friendly Proposal to prevent Murder and other enormous Abuses, By erecting an Hospital for Foundlings and Bastard-Children. With a full Answer to all Objections yet brought against that laudable Undertaking. Also to save many Persons from Destruction, by clearing the Streets of Shameless Strumpets, suppressing Gaming-Tables, and Sunday Debauches: With a plain Explosion of, and Proposal to amend a growing Abuse, viz. the barbarous Custom of Men's putting their Wives into private Mad-houses, on frivolous Pretences, where they often end their Days in utmost Misery. Also a Proposal to amend several great Abuses daily committed by Watermen. And necessary Hints for redressing divers other publick Grievances, which call aloud for Amendment. Humbly Dedicated to the Right Honourable Humphry Parsons, Esq. Lord-Mayor of the City of London. And highly worthy the Consideration of the Legislature. London, 1731.

Of Royall Educacion. A Fragmentary Treatise. First published in 1895.

BIBLIOGRAPHY

The writings of Defoe which are concerned with, or allude to education, are to be found in the Appendix. Secondary sources are listed below either as books or articles.

Abbreviations used: E.C.S. *Eighteenth Century Studies*
J.H.I. *Journal of History of Ideas*
R.E.S. *Review of English Studies*

Books

(a) *Eighteenth Century—General Works*

Clark, G. N., *The Later Stuarts 1660-1714*, Oxford University Press, 1949.

Cragg, Gerald R., *The Church and the Age of Reason 1648-1789*, Penguin Books, Harmondsworth Press, 1976.

Dennis, John, *The Age of Pope*, Bell, 1896.

Foss, Michael, *The Age of Patronage*, Hamish Hamilton, 1971.

Greene, Donald, *The Age of Exuberance*, Random House, 1970.

Hill, Christopher, *The Century of Revolution 1603-1714*, Sphere Books, 1969.

Humphreys, A. R., *The Augustan World*, Methuen, 1954.

Lonsdale, Roger (Ed.), *Dryden to Johnson*, Sphere Books, 1971.

Mingay, G. E., *English Landed Society in the Eighteenth Century*, Routledge and Kegan Paul, 1963.

Plumb, J. H., *England in the Eighteenth Century*, Pelican, Harmondsworth Press, 1950.

Plumb, J. H. and Dearing, V. A., *Some Aspects of Eighteenth-Century England*, University of California, Los Angeles, 1971.

Rudé, George, *Europe in the Eighteenth Century*, Sphere Books, 1974.

Saintsbury, George, *The Peace of the Augustans*, Bell, 1916.

Stephen, Leslie, *English Literature and Society in the Eighteenth Century*, Duckworth, 1904.

Turberville, A. S., *English Men and Manners in the Eighteenth Century*, Oxford University Press, 1926.

Williams, Basil, *The Whig Supremacy*, Oxford University Press, 1952.

(b)   *Eighteenth Century—Education*

Adamson, J. W., *Pioneers of Modern Education 1600-1700*, Cambridge University Press, 1905.

Dobbs, A. E., *Educational and Social Movements 1700-1850*, Longmans, Green and Co., 1919.

Hans, N., *New Trends in Education in the Eighteenth Century*, Routledge and Kegan Paul, 1951.

Jarman, T. L., *Landmarks in the History of Education*, Murray, 1963.

Jones, M. G., *The Charity School Movement*, Frank Cass, 1964.

Lowther Clark, W. K., *A History of the S.P.C.K.*, S.P.C.K., 1959.

McLachlan, H., *English Education under the Test Acts*, Manchester University Press, 1931.

Montmorency, J. E. G., *State Intervention in English Education*, Cambridge University Press, 1902.

Neuburg, V. E., *Popular Education in Eighteenth-Century England*, Woburn Press, 1971.

Ogilvie, R. M., *Latin and Greek*, Routledge and Kegan Paul, 1964.

Parker, Irene, *Dissenting Academies in England*, Cambridge University Press, 1914.

Smith, J. W. Ashley, *The Birth of Modern Education: The Contribution of The Dissenting Academies 1660-1800*, Independent Press, 1954.

Watson, Forster, *The Beginnings of the Teaching of Modern Subjects in England*, Pitman, 1909.

Wordsworth, Christopher, *Scholae Academicae*, Frank Cass, 1968.

(c)   *Bibliographies or Commentaries on Daniel Defoe*

Baine, R. M., *Daniel Defoe and the Supernatural*, University of Georgia Press, 1968.

Boulton, J. T. (Ed.), *Selected Writings of Daniel Defoe*, Cambridge University Press, 1975.

Chadwick, W., *The Life and Times of Daniel Defoe*, J. R. Smith, 1859.

Chalmers, G., *The Life of Daniel Defoe*, J. Stockdale, 1790.

Dudley, Edward and Novak, M. E., *The Wild Man Within*, University of Pittsburg Press, 1972.

Earle, Peter, *The World of Defoe*, Weidenfeld and Nicolson, 1976.

Ellis, F. H. (Ed.), *Twentieth Century Interpretations of Robinson Crusoe*, Prentice Hall, 1969.

Fitzgerald, Brian, *Daniel Defoe: a Study in Conflict*, Secker and Warburg, 1954.

Freeman, W., *The Incredible De Foe*, Herbert Jenkins, 1950.

Healey, G. H. (Ed.), *The Letters of Daniel Defoe*, Oxford University Press, 1955.

Hunter, J. Paul, *The Reluctant Pilgrim: Defoe's Emblematic Method and Quest for Form in Robinson Crusoe*, The Johns Hopkins Press, 1966.

Lee, William, *Daniel Defoe: His Life and Recently Discovered Writings*, London, 1869. Reprinted, Hildesheim, 1968.

Minto, W., *Daniel Defoe*, MacMillan, 1902.

Moore, J. R., *A Checklist of the Writings of Daniel Defoe*, 2nd Edition, Archon, 1971.

Moore, J. R., *Defoe in the Pillory, and other Studies*, Bloomington, Indiana, 1939.

Moore, J. R., *Daniel Defoe: Citizen of the Modern World*, University of Chicago Press, 1958.

Novak, M. E., *Defoe and the Nature of Man*, Oxford University Press, 1963.

Novak, M. E., *Economics and the Fiction of Daniel Defoe*, Berkeley & Los Angeles, 1962.

Payne, W. L., *Index to Defoe's Review*, Columbia University Press, 1948.

Payne, W. L. (Ed.), *The Best of Defoe's Review: An Anthology*, Columbia University Press, 1951.

Primer, Irwin (Ed.), *Mandeville Studies*, Martinus Nijhoff, The Hague, 1975 (includes essay by J. R. Moore—Mandeville and Defoe, pp. 119-25).

Rogers, Pat, *The Augustan Vision*, Weidenfeld and Nicolson, 1974.

Rogers, Pat (Ed.), *Defoe: the Critical Heritage*, Routledge and Kegan Paul, 1972.

Rogers, Pat, *Grub Street: Studies in a Subculture*, Methuen, 1972.

Secord, A. W., *Studies in the Narrative Method of Defoe*, Urbana, Illinois, 1924.

Shinagel, Michael, *Daniel Defoe and Middle-Class Gentility*, Harvard University Press, 1968.

Starr, G. A., *Defoe and Casuistry*, Princeton University Press, 1971.

Starr, G. A., *Defoe and Spiritual Autobiography*, Princeton University Press, 1965.

Sutherland, J. R., *Defoe*, Methuen, 1937.

Sutherland, James, *Daniel Defoe*, Harvard University Press, 1971.

Trent, W. P., *Daniel Defoe: How to Know Him*, Indianapolis, 1916.

Watson, Francis, *Daniel Defoe*, Longmans Green and Co., 1952.

Watt, I., *The Rise of the Novel*, Chatto and Windus, 1957.

Wilson, R. (Ed.), *The Arts in Society*, Prentice Hall, 1967. (Ian Watt: Robinson Crusoe as a Myth.)

Wilson, Walter, *Memoirs of the Life and Times of Daniel De Foe*, 3 vols., London, 1830.

Articles

A correspondent, Who Founded London University? Daniel Defoe's Claim, *Times Educational Supplement*, July 11, 1936.

Bishop, Jonathan, Knowledge, Action and Interpretation in Defoe's Novels, *J.H.I.*, XIII, No. 1. January 1952.

Burch, C. E., Daniel Defoe's Views on Education, *London Quarterly Review*, 1930.

Burch, C. E., Defoe and the Edinburgh Society for the Reformation of Manners, *R.E.S.*, Vol. 16, No. 63, July 1940.

Clinton, K. B., Femme et Philosophe: Enlightenment Origins of Feminism, *E.C.S.*, Vol. 8, No. 3, Spring 1975.

Downie, J. A., Daniel Defoe and the General Election of 1708 in Scotland, *E.C.S.*, Vol. 8, No. 3, Spring 1975.

Girdler, L., Defoe's Education at Newington Green Academy, *Studies in Philology*, Vol. 50, 1953.

Ivanyi, B. G., Defoe's Prelude to the Family Instructor, *Times Literary Supplement*, April 7, 1966.

Macaree, David, Daniel Defoe, the Church of Scotland and the Union of 1707, *E.C.S.*, Vol. 7, No. 1, Fall 1973.

McBurney, W., Colonel Jacque: Defoe's definition of the Complete English Gentleman, *Studies in English Literature*, Vol. 2, 1962.

Leinster-Mackay, D. P., A Review of the Affairs of France: a continuity factor in Defoe's interest in English education, *Paedagogica Historica*, XVI/2, 1976.

Leinster-Mackay, D. P., Daniel Defoe: an eighteenth century educationist? *Education Research and Perspectives*, Vol. 5, No. 2, June 1978.

Leinster-Mackay, D. P., Daniel Defoe—the great projector: a consideration of the ideas of Defoe for the improvement of English education, *History of Education Society Bulletin*, No. 25, Spring 1980.

Leinster-Mackay, D. P., Regina v Hopley. Some historical reflections on corporal punishment. *Journal of Educational Administration and History*, Vol. IX, No. 1, January 1977.

Leinster-Mackay, D. P., Rousseau and Defoe: a case of misguided advocacy or paradox par excellence in eighteenth century education? *Journal of Educational Thought* (University of Calgary), Vol. 13, No. 2, August 1979.

Novak, Maximillian E., Defoe's "Indifferent Monitor," The Complexity of Moll Flanders, *E.C.S.*, Vol. 3, No. 3, Spring 1970.

Rogers, Pat, Literary Art in Defoe's *Tour*: The Rhetoric of Growth and Decay, *E.C.S.*, Vol. 6, No. 2, Winter 1972-73.

Starr, G. A., From Casuistry to Fiction: the Importance of the *Altenian Mercury*, *J.H.I.*, Vol. 28, No. 1, 1967.

Watt, I., The Recent Critical Fortunes of *Moll Flanders*, *E.C.S.*, Vol. 1, No. 1, September 1967.